1000 Stranger Things Facts

by Joe Ellroy

1000 Stranger Things Facts contains all the trivia you could ever wish to know about the smash hit Netflix series. The cast and crew, special effects, food, fashions, cars, monsters, characters, props, shooting locations, influences, music, behind the scenes anecdotes, auditions, eighties technology, anachronisms and goofs, and much more. Get ready to unlock the curiosity door and enjoy one thousand facts all about Stranger Things...

(1) Eleven actress Millie Bobby Brown is deaf in one ear.

(2) The original title of Stranger Things was Montauk. "It was originally set in Montauk," said co-creator Matt Duffer. "Jaws was our favorite movie of all time, so we liked the sort of coastal setting that that allowed, but for production reasons it started to look more and more unfeasible."

(3) Montauk was the location of a conspiracy theory that sowed some of the seeds for the plot of what would become Stranger Things. Montauk Air Force Station on Montauk, Long Island, was - some allege - the home of a secret government project to investigate psychological warfare, time travel, quantum fields, and telekinesis.

(4) In Stranger Things 2, episode five Dig Dug, there is a mistake when Erica Sinclair is seen using Butterworth syrup on her French toast. Erica is using a plastic bottle that you squeeze but in 1984 the syrup was still in a glass container. Plastic bottles were not introduced until 1999.

(5) The character of Steve Harrington - the teen villain for most of season one - was much more unpleasant in the original conception for Stranger Things. However, when the Duffers noticed the charm and comic timing of actor Joe Keery they decided to change the story arc of Steve so they could use

this side of Keery in the show. By the end of season one, Steve has atoned for most of his sins and in season two he becomes a hero when he babysits the children.

(6) Gaten Matarazzo read for the part of Mike but was eventually given the role of Dustin. The Duffers said that the part of Dustin was changed so that it would be tailor made for Matarazzo. "We didn't really even know who the Dustin character was until we found Gaten. He was sort of a generic nerd with glasses kind of a character - he was a stereotype. He was not a three-dimensional character. And then we saw Gaten's take, we fell in love with this kid, flew him out to Los Angeles, and met him. Gaten completely informed that character."

(7) Ross Duffer says the immense fame that Stranger Things has given the child actors does make them (the Duffers) worry a little. "It's surreal for us, but even more so for them. I walk down the street, and no one cares, but when we're wandering around with the kids, everyone comes up to them. It's certainly a surreal experience, and it's hard for me to know exactly how they're coping with it. I just know that on set, the kids are the same. They still seem like normal kids, which is what I worried about coming into this season. But they seem to be pretty well-grounded and handling it very well."

(8) Ross Duffer says Stranger Things is more inspired by Stephen King than Steven Spielberg. "Obviously Spielberg's getting thrown around a lot and that's great, but also it's exciting that this is Netflix and not a movie, and that's why we put the chapter title cards on every episode. We wanted it to feel like you're sitting down and reading this big fat Stephen King book and that was exciting to us. Because this is something sprawling, we can tell this story over a much longer period of time than two hours. So inherently it's going to have a different texture and taste to it than, say, a Spielberg movie or what not, so that works for the Stephen King

references that are coming in."

(9) The Duffers played spooky music on the set to get the actors in the right mood to convey fear and tension for scary scenes. During the mist blanketed junkyard sequence in Stranger Things 2 the crew played the Close Encounters soundtrack.

(10) Millie Bobby Brown did not enjoy being kissed by Finn Wolfhard when Mike kisses Eleven in the first season finale. When the director yelled "cut!", Brown declared that "kissing sucks!", much to the amusement of Wolfhard and the crew.

(11) Winona Ryder, who plays Joyce Byers, spent a few years in a commune with no electricity as a child.

(12) Ryder's godfather was counterculture icon Timothy Leary. Leary was famous for advocating the spiritual benefits of LSD.

(13) Netflix wanted to shoot seasons two and three of Stranger Things back to back so the children would not appear to age but the Duffers vetoed this plan as they felt that it would put too much strain on the writing and production of the show. The Duffers also felt that the fact that the young cast members were constantly changing and growing up fast was not necessarily a bad thing and made the show more interesting.

(14) The Duffers say that they kept Eleven away from the boys in season two to take away their own safety net. "That's probably the biggest difference for this season, in that Eleven is not with the boys, really. I mean, you know, there were conversations with Netflix. Everyone was nervous about it just because a lot of the success of the first season came from her interaction with the boys — the chemistry between them. And then immediately, you're kind of taking away that safety net. And I think that part of that was just to challenge

ourselves. We really wanted to not do the same thing again. ... we wanted her to have her own journey, separate from the boys."

(15) The Hugh Jackman film Prisoners, a thriller about a missing child, was an unlikely influence on Stranger Things. The Duffers watched this film and had the idea of taking a broadly similar premise and giving it a sci-fi/horror twist.

(16) There are many visual homages to films and directors the Duffers love in Stranger Things. To give some examples, the scene at the start of the very first episode where the scientist looks up in the elevator and is pulled up by an unseen monster is based on a similar shot in David Fincher's Alien 3. Another homage comes when Eleven shows recognition when she looks a photograph of Will early on in season one. This is a reference to a scene in Peter Weir's Witness.

(17) Charlie Heaton, who plays Jonathan Byers, used to be a drummer in a band called Comanechi (who became a modest minor cult in Britain through their eccentric singer Akiko Matsuura). "In all seriousness, it's been incredible," said Heaton in 2013. "From leaving college – not that I attended that often – to touring with the likes of Gossip and Bo Ningen, and within a month of joining the band playing in front of over 3,000 people, it's been pretty mental. I didn't expect it." In 2015, Heaton left the world of music and took up acting. Stranger Things soon followed.

(18) Although Noah Schnapp hardly features in season one with Will trapped in the Upside Down, he was cast because they knew he was talented enough to play the major role they had planned for him in season two. Schnapp was described by producer Shawn Levy as "a Ferrari sitting in the garage" in season one.

(19) The Duffers got around fifteen rejections when they first

pitched Stranger Things to networks. The networks were not convinced that a show largely based around children would work or appeal to adults.

(20) David Harbour nearly quit acting not long before Stranger Things. He was frustrated at his treatment in Hollywood. The part of Chief Hopper was the first time that anyone had made Harbour a leading man.

(21) Eleven says only 246 words in the first season of Stranger Things.

(22) The actress who played her, Shannon Purser, said she was surprised by the 'Justice for Barb' movement and the fact that the character became so cultish despite being killed off relatively early in the show. "It still blows me away that she got the kind of response that she did. A lot of it, I think, is timing. I think a lot of people definitely relate to the people who are less than conventional — at least by Hollywood standards — people who are an outcast and awkward, because more often than not, we don't feel like the cool, popular kid who had everything together in high school. Most of us have been a third wheel or have been stuck at a party we didn't want to be at. I think there's definitely this fondness about Barb and her situation because we've all been there before."

(23) Shannon Purser said she actually enjoyed shooting Barb's death in the Upside Down infected swimming pool. "That was definitely an adventure. I think it was also my favourite day of shooting, getting to do that scene, because as an actor, you don't really have anything to go off of, and you're screaming at the top of your lungs. It was a challenge, but it was really cool to get into that emotional place, and I'm really proud of myself for pulling it off because I definitely wasn't sure at first. The set was super cool. Even though I'm sure there was editing done, it looked very convincing. There were these

gross vines everywhere, and they put glycerin and slime all over the whole set, which was both disgusting and cool. They did have little spores and stuff floating it the air. That was really awesome."

(24) Hopper's trailer home in season one was purchased by the production staff for the paltry sum of one dollar.

(25) For the scene where Eleven descends into the sensory deprivation water tank in the laboratory, Millie Bobby Brown wore a real life Sea Trek helmet which weighed approximately 70 pounds.

(26) Gaten Matarazzo, who plays Dustin Henderson, has cleidocranial dysplasia, a condition which means his teeth have yet to come through. The 'pearls' that Dustin is so proud of in Stranger Things 2 are dentures.

(27) Computer games have been a notable influence on Stranger Things. The Duffers have cited Dark Souls, Silent Hill and the Uncharted series as games they used for inspiration.

(28) Stephen King singled out Millie Bobby Brown for praise on his Twitter stream when she acted in the BBC America series Intruders. Quite prophetic given that Brown's breakout role would later come in a show inspired by his books.

(29) Joe Chrest, who plays Ted Wheeler, is also a music professor in real life.

(30) Finn Wolfhard was ill during the auditions so filmed his audition in his bed.

(31) Millie Bobby Brown says that whenever the boys started to irritate her on the set in season one she would go to Winona Ryder's trailer and eat cheese with her.

(32) The Duffers were so determined to get Paul Reiser to play Dr Owens in Stranger Things 2 that the character - who had yet to be named - was known as 'Dr Reiser' in the early script.

(33) Charlie Heaton and Natalia Dyer, who play lovebirds Jonathan and Nancy, found romance together in real life too when it was confirmed in 2017 that they were dating.

(34) Although Millie Bobby Brown and Noah Schnapp are best friends in real life they don't have a single proper dialogue scene with one another in the entire first two seasons of Stranger Things.

(35) Millie Bobby Brown says that she can tolerate eggo waffles in real life but doesn't like having to eat too many of them. She likes blueberry ones the best.

(36) Dacre Montgomery, who plays the angry Billy Hargrove, caught the eye in his audition tape by dancing to Duran Duran. "I made a little short film, with an opening score and title credits and I read both of the scenes I was given...I danced in a g-string to Hungry Like The Wolf. I'm a fan of going against the grain. That audition could have gone one of two ways. I could have never worked in this industry again, but someone, somewhere, saw something."

(37) The Demogorgon in season one is played by Mark Steger in a monster suit although there was also CGI used at times to depict the creature. The Duffers wanted the monster to seem like a real life practical beast rather than a special effect. It was inspired by Bolaji Badejo wearing the alien suit to play the monster in Ridley Scott's 1979 classic Alien.

(38) Paul Lester, a former employee of the energy department, wrote an article after Stranger Things came out in which he talked about all the good things that the energy department do in their work and reminded us that Stranger Things'

depiction of the energy department as an evil secret government agency meddling with monsters and super powered children wasn't completely accurate! For the record, Lester said that he enjoyed the show very much though. Here's some of his article - 'Stranger Things depicts the Energy Department as a federal agency confronting terrifying monsters lurking in different dimensions. We don't mess with monsters, but the Energy Department is in the business of detecting invisible dangers. Energy Department scientists throughout the country create new technologies that help prevent terrorists from getting their hands on nuclear materials. For example, Sandia National Laboratories developed a mobile scanner that can be used in shipping ports around the world to quickly detect radiological materials hidden inside massive cargo containers.'

(39) Second season director Andrew Stanton says working on the show made him feel very nostalgic and that he was impressed by the accuracy of the period recreations by the art and costume departments. "I was 15 to 25 in the 1980s. I went to college, studied film, went to the movies like crazy and ate everything up. The Duffers captured exactly what it was like to watch all that stuff. There's a pure sense of wonder about the show, and an appreciation for unadulterated geek cinema. Family Feud was mine. The songs are a separate thing. But really, the Duffers trust their art department and props department and set-dressing department and costume department to go on little archaeological digs. I haven't talked about this with the Duffers or with Shawn (Levy), but I have to believe that half the fun of directing an episode of Stranger Things, for them, is walking onto the set and suddenly seeing the extras wearing those clothes and seeing all the vintage props and getting inspired by what's in front of you. That surprise is really useful."

(40) The password to enter Will's woodland clubhouse 'Castle Byers' is Radagast. Radagast is a wizard in Lord of the Rings.

(41) Holly Wheeler is played by twins Anniston and Tinsley Price. The twins also played baby Judith in season four of The Walking Dead.

(42) Winona Ryder had no idea what streaming meant when it was explained to her that the show would be on Netflix. She said she rarely used a computer.

(43) The sequence where Eleven makes the scientist van flip over the children on their bicycles in The Bathtub was very complicated and costly to shoot. The stunt had to be staged twice to get it perfect.

(44) Joe Keery thinks there might be a homoerotic frisson behind the rivalry of Steve and Billy Hargrove in season two. Dacre Montgomery is not so convinced though and says Billy is a "ladies man".

(45) In the original script for Stranger Things, Eleven was supposed to die for good in the finale after vanquishing the Demogorgon. When a second season was seen as inevitable they decided to change this plan and make her apparent demise more ambiguous so that the character could return.

(46) Millie Bobby Brown didn't enjoy shooting the scenes of Eleven alone in the cabin in Stranger Things 2. She much prefers having other actors to bounce off.

(47) After they abandoned plans to set the show in Montauk, the Duffers put off giving the show a new name because they couldn't think of one that sounded right. When they eventually considered 'Stranger Things' as a new title they decided that it was apt enough to use.

(48) David Harbour said it was wonderful to work with Winona Ryder because he had been a fan of her since the

eighties when he first saw the film Heathers.

(49) David Harbour had his hair cut into a mowhawk when Stranger Things 2 began production so had to wear a hairpiece.

(50) Noah Schnapp also wore a hairpiece in Stranger Things 2. His own hair was too short for Will's signature 'bowl cut'.

(51) Gaten Matarazzo says that Charlie Heaton is the worst (in a nice way) person to do a scene with in Stranger Things because they always end up laughing and having to do multiple takes.

(52) There is an anachronism when Barb is seen driving a Volkswagen Cabrio in season one. Although season one is set in 1983, Barb's car is a 1988 model.

(53) Chief Jim Hopper drives a 1980 Chevrolet K5 Blazer in the show.

(54) The camera that Jonathan Byers uses is a Pentax MX.

(55) In 'The Bathtub' episode, Mr Clarke is seen at home watching John Carpenter's The Thing. This seems like a mistake as season one is set in 1983 and The Thing was not released on VHS until 1984. Surely Mr Clarke would not have a pirate bootleg copy!

(56) Will's cassette player is a Panasonic RX-5090 Boombox.

(57) Joyce Byers has a Western Electric 554 Yellow Wall Phone.

(58) The television set in the Wheeler house is a 22-inch Mitsubishi.

(59) Bob Newby's video camera in Stranger Things 2 is a JVC

GR-C1. This was the same one that Michael J Fox used in Back to the Future.

(60) Nancy and Barb - best friends in season one before the early demise of Barb - seem to have names inspired by 1980s first ladies Nancy Reagan and Barbara Bush.

(61) The Demogorgon figurine in Mike's basement den was not produced until 1984.

(62) The eagle eyed bike enthusiasts who watched the show were confused why the lights on the boys bikes seemed to be orange during daylight sequences in season one. Orange lights were not used on bikes in the eighties. The mystery was solved when it was deduced that the orange 'lights' were orange gels. They were used by the production designers so the bike lights could be altered to match the production lights at night and no undesired hues could occur.

(63) The name of the character Jonathan Byers is seen as a possible tribute/reference to John Fitzgerald Byers, one of the 'Lone Gunmen' in The X-Files.

(64) Charlie Heaton missed the Stranger Things 2 premiere because he was detained at LAX airport with a small amount of cocaine. Heaton was not arrested but was refused entry to the United States and put on a flight back to Britain. He released this statement: "My planned travel to the U.S. last week was affected by an issue at U.S. immigration, and I am working to rectify it as soon as possible. I do want to clarify that I was not arrested or charged with a crime, and cooperated fully with the U.S. officials at LAX. I'm sorry to all the fans and my Stranger Things family for missing the premiere. We are all so proud of this season and I would never want this story to negatively impact the show."

(65) Millie Bobby Brown was signed by IMG models in 2017

and has done a shoot for Calvin Klein amongst others.

(66) Sadie Sink had to work with a skateboarding instructor for three hours a day to play the skateboarding Max.

(67) Natalia Dyer has combined Stranger Things with studying at New York University. She studied at NYU's Gallatin School of Individualized Study.

(68) Noah Schnapp did so much screaming in the Stranger Things 2 finale he lost his voice for three days.

(69) Noah Schnapp and Winona Ryder unsuccessfully lobbied the Duffers to not kill off Bob Newby in Stranger Things 2 because they loved working with Sean Astin so much.

(70) Sean Astin and Winona Ryder were very close on the set as they had much in common. Both began their careers as eighties child stars.

(71) In the season two episode The Lost Sister, the Chicago skyline we see contains buildings which didn't exist in 1984. The Trump International Hotel & Tower opened in 2009 and the Blue Cross Blue Shield Tower opened in 1997.

(72) 361,000 people watched all nine episodes of Stranger Things 2 within the first 24 hours of its release.

(73) In three days, Stranger Things 2 had fifteen million viewers streaming it.

(74) Netflix was founded by by Reed Hastings and Marc Randolph in 1997. They began in the DVD rental market and expanded to streaming in 2010. They entered the content-production industry with House of Cards in 2013.

(75) Video arcade games in the 1980s used cathode ray tube

(CRT) monitors - not flat-panel LCD screens as seen in the arcade scenes in Stranger Things 2.

(76) Gaten Matarazzo made his stage debut in Priscilla, Queen of the Desert in 2011. In 2014 he played Gavroche/Petit Gervaisin Les Misérables at the Imperial Theatre in midtown-Manhattan.

(77) Millie Bobby Brown is a supporter of Liverpool football (soccer) team.

(78) The state trooper that Hopper punches in the episode titled The Body is reading Stephen King's 1981 novel Cujo.

(79) Dr Brenner was described in the early scripts as wearing a shirt and jeans. Matthew Modine was allowed to make some changes to the character and had the idea of making Brenner more regimented and aloof. Modine felt Brenner would be the sort of person who wore a dark plain suit each day.

(80) Charlie Heaton accidentally punched Joe Keery twice for real during the alley fight between Jonathan and Steve in the first season.

(81) 1,200 pounds of epsom salt were used in the kiddie pool when Eleven floats in the hastily constructed deprivation chamber constructed in the school.

(82) Stranger Things uses three songs by Tangerine Dream in episodes. Tangerine Dream are most famous for their eighties movie scores. In 2017, Tangerine Dream started doing a cover of the Stranger Things theme in their set as a tribute.

(83) Millie Bobby Brown briefly held up production of season one when she turned up for work one morning covered in glitter. The Duffers said it was moments like this that reminded them of how young the kids in the show were.

(84) Stephen King is a big fan of the King inspired show. He called it 'Steve King's greatest hits'.

(85) The fame of Stranger Things is such that it was the subject of an affectionate Sesame Street parody in 2017. It features Cookie Monster as the Cookiegorgon!

(86) It took Mark Steger half an hour to get into the Demogorgon suit.

(87) It took 26 motors to work the 'petal flesh' head of the Demogorgon.

(88) Mark Steger wore stilts to convey the large size of the monster and the long arms were operated by puppeteers.

(89) Dustin's love of Three Musketeers candy is a twist on kids usually being disappointed at Halloween if they get too many of them. Three Musketeers is a candy bar consisting of whipped nougat with a chocolate covering. Many feel that a Three Musketeers is just a Snickers with all the good stuff taken out!

(90) Noah Schnapp supports the Montreal Canadiens ice hockey team.

(91) Mike Wheeler has a poster for Jim Henson's eighties fantasy film The Dark Crystal on his wall.

(92) Winona Ryder says the thing she loved about Stranger Things was playing a character who was her own age. "For me, I'm finally getting to play my own age, and it's liberating. I would not want to go back to playing the ingénue. I'm not someone like Norma Desmond who's harking back to her younger days."

(93) Winona Ryder said she had to cry for real in Stranger Things because she's allergic to the chemical they use to make actors tear up.

(94) Winona Ryder says that she worries a little about the younger cast members of Stranger Things and the fame and intrusion they face in the modern age. "I'm grateful that I got to start at the time I did. As much as I love it, I don't know if I would even have become an actor [if I was starting out now]. I wouldn't know how to [handle it]. I do worry about the massive exposure at that age."

(95) David Harbour says that he 'ships' Hopper and Joyce. "The fans they call it like 'Jopper' or something, they all ship this relationship with Hopper and Joyce and I do too, because I feel like they're two really lonely, lost people that really need each other. I sort of have always seen their relationship kind of like Chinatown with Faye Dunaway and Jack Nicholson."

(96) David Harbour binge-watched Stranger Things when it first aired just like everyone else. "I couldn't stop watching... I knew what was coming, but I will say I got lost in it to the point where — and this is sad and pathetic — I was on my couch in the East Village watching the scene where I'm saving Will and I'm crying on my couch, going, 'He saved that little boy.' I forgot completely that it was me, that I was involved in the show. I was just drunk on [creators Matt and Ross] Duffer magic. I love the show and I'm so rarely proud of things that I do. I see all the flaws [in my work]. It really is those creators and directors that are true geniuses … they just elevate it."

(97) David Harbour says the kids on the show were quite challenging to work with. "I was joking before but it's the farting that goes on with 12-year-olds. The amount of bodily functions they can't control is amazing. It's all kinds of boogers. When you go to work you should not have to deal with someone like — yeah, it was bad. Also now they're

growing up, now they're 13, 14 and you know what happens then, right? The hormones, hair growing. It's like weird to watch a human being develop. There are little moments of weirdness. It's great and it's horrible because you want to sort of get your workday done and they're sort of crazy children."

(98) At the Critics' Choice Awards, David Harbour expressed his affection for Millie Bobby Brown and his hopes for her future. "My hope with Millie has and is always that she will be an artist, that when I am in the nursing home, she will bring me her Oscars. But, I feel like the pitfalls are very deep in terms of this generation; this fame, this Instagram generation of constantly wanting to get likes. I never really grew up with that and the fact that there is somebody with eleven million followers or something like, that's thinking about their persona to the world at thirteen or fourteen years of age is terrifying to me. I know she has tremendous potential and my hope is that she can remain grounded and protected as much as possible. I'm protective of her. I want her to grow up to become Meryl Steep. I don't want her in rehab at 20, or whatever, because she's a child star. I know she's super talented, but they all were talented and there is this trajectory of tension and spotlight placed on a young, developing person, which, to me, is terrifying, seen through parental eyes."

(99) In season one, a copy of Hanz Holzer's book Great American Ghost Stories can be seen on a shelf. This is a mistake because the book was published in 1990.

(100) The Upside Down was called the Nether in the Stranger Things season one scripts.

(101) When some of the cast and crew visited the White House after the first season they learned that President Obama was a big fan of the show.

(102) Although the Stranger Things score is heavily inspired by the synth movie scores of John Carpenter, Carpenter himself has said he doesn't see the connection personally. "I saw a preview of Stranger Things — I haven't watched it. It didn't sound anything like me. And I'm not sure which ones people are talking about. As far as I can see, nobody scores movies like I do. They just don't. They don't even try to do it the way I do it, which is fine. If you point out something to me, I'll take a listen to it."

(103) The Stranger Things title theme sounds incredibly like Wanna Fight from the Only God Forgives soundtrack by Cliff Martinez. Have a listen and see what you think.

(104) The Wheeler family are eating chicken, tater tots, dinner rolls, and mixed vegetables when we see them eat dinner early on in Stranger Things.

(105) The producer Shawn Levy said that getting permission to use Michael Jackson's thriller for the Stranger Things 2 trailer was very complicated. "Getting Thriller for the season-two trailer took months. We tried 50 other songs. Literally, I'd wake up at 4 a.m. thinking, "It's a good trailer, but it's not going to make people lose their mother-effing minds." So without telling the brothers, I went back into it with the lawyers for Michael Jackson's estate, which was complicated by factors I won't go into right now. Suffice it to say, it was a big group of people that had to come to a yes."

(106) The Duffers toyed with the idea of season two skipping to the present day very early on in the development of Stranger Things but ultimately decided to jettison this idea.

(107) Most of the networks who rejected Stranger Things wanted the show to lose the kids and focus on Hopper as the central character.

(108) Millie Bobby Brown did not enjoy shooting the scene where Eleven sneaks into Benny's Burgers in the first episode. "Oh, that was the worst day in the world! I had to stuff my face with cold fries. They were so greasy. I had like three burgers, and I'd put them in my mouth, and they were cold. I was like, are you kidding me? I had a cup beside me, and I would say "Eleven," and then I would spit the burger into the cup and come back up. There's a blooper take where I just spit it right out. Everyone starts laughing."

(109) 90% of the spores you see floating around in the Upside Down scenes in Stranger Things are digital.

(110) Millie Bobby Brown's hair had grown out when they made Stranger Things 2 and so to recreate her season one look in the flashback in episode two (to show how Eleven escaped from the Upside Down) they used CGI to replicate Eleven's buzzcut.

(111) Visual effects producer Christina Graff explained the concept of the 'Shadow Monster' in season two. "We knew from the Duffers that it would be humongous, like 50 stories tall. Since we had all these electrical disturbances last year in season one, where the Christmas lights were blinking or any sort of electrical light is blinking, we knew there were going to be storms in season two. The Shadow Monster is somehow connected to all of that energy, and then we determined it's gonna be like cloud-like or storm-like. We had conversations also with the production designer, Chris Trujillo, and we searched for a lot of references to storms and clouds and things like tornadoes."

(112) The Shadow Monster was largely inspired by volcanic eruptions and lightning storms.

(113) It took a month to design the models for how the Demogorgon would look in Stranger Things.

(114) Although the show is set in Indiana it is filmed just outside of Atlanta in Georgia.

(115) Shawn Levy had to contact the director Ivan Reitman to get permission to use Ghostbusters costumes in season two.

(116) A 27 year-old female model named Ali Michael sparked controversy in 2017 when she made an Instagram post asking Stranger Things actor Finn Wolfhard to "hit me up in four years." Wolfhard was fourteen years old at the time and Michael was slammed for her inappropriate comments regarding a minor. She made the following statement: "It was never my intention (nor has it ever been) to sexualize a minor in any way shape or form. To those I offended or misled, I apologise for a post made in haste and lacking in sensitivity, particularly considering the landscape of the present culture."

(117) Millie Bobby Brown wants Hopper and Joyce to get together in future seasons because that would mean she might get some scenes with Noah Schnapp.

(118) Hopper's police uniform is inspired by that of Chief Brody in Steven Spielberg's Jaws. The Duffer Brothers have said that Jaws is their most beloved film.

(119) Natalia Dyer says she doesn't like horror films in real life but she did enjoy A Nightmare On Elm Street when she watched some eighties movies. The name Nancy might possibly be inspired by the heroine of A Nightmare On Elm Street.

(120) Finn Wolfhard is the lead singer for a Vancouver band named Calpurnia. The band were signed to an album deal and got a good review in the famous British music paper NME.

(121) Finn says his dream is to jam with Paul McCartney.

(122) In Dungeons & Dragons, Mind Flayers are monsters known as illithids. They have psionic powers and want to control all dimensions.

(123) Millie Bobby Brown says she swiped two props from the set when Stranger Things season one finished production. Some of the fake blood (for Eleven's nosebleeds) and Eleven's fake 011 tattoo.

(124) The stereo belonging to Jonathan Byers is a Fisher MC-4550 from 1981.

(125) The TRC-214 walkie-talkies in Stranger Things might be a slight mistake as they only started being listed in Radio Shack's 1985 catalogue - two years after season one takes place.

(126) Because they don't make chocolate puddings in metal cans anymore, the props department put chocolate pudding labels on metal tins of luncheon meat.

(127) Dacre Montgomery says he based the character of Billy Hargrove on real life bullies he had known growing up in Australia.

(128) Joyce Byers drives a 1976 Ford Pinto.

(129) Jonathan Byers drives an early seventies Ford LTD.

(130) The Hawkins Energy Department use Chevy Vans.

(131) You can tell that Steve Harrington's family is rich because he drives a BMW 733i.

(132) The real location for Hawkins Police Station in Stranger Things is 48 Pray Street in Douglasville, Georgia.

(133) When Brett Galman as Murray Bauman drops some scrambled egg from his fork having breakfast with Nancy and Jonathan and you see Natalia Dyer and Charlie Heaton try not to laugh, this was a real mistake that they decided to keep in because they thought it was a funny scene.

(134) The Lost sister is the only episode of Stranger Things that met a mixed to negative reception in reviews.

(135) It was always the dream of the Duffer Brothers to make a big screen adaptation of Stephen King's It. They did not get their wish but - in a quirk of fate - Stranger Things star Finn Wolfhard starred in the film when 'IT' was adapted in 2017.

(136) Gaten Matarazzo and Noah Schnapp both read for the part of Mike Wheeler but were given other roles.

(137) The 'teenagers' in Stranger Things are played by actors too old for high school. Joe Keery and Charlie Heaton, for example, were both already in their twenties when they made season one.

(138) Noah Schnapp is a rarity in that he plays a character slightly older than his real age.

(139) Amy L Forsythe, head of the makeup department for Stranger Things, said they used white frosting and food colouring to make Will's tongue look green in Stranger Things 2 when he is ill. They then found out that Noah Schnapp hates frosting!

(140) How did the makeup department create the mud splattered faces of those who endure the Upside Down tunnels? "We had a mud that we really liked, kind of like clays and that kind of stuff, but it didn't quite have the texture that I wanted, and I wanted more textural layers to it. So, we were

playing in the trailer, and we have an espresso machine in the trailer, so I took our concoction and I threw in the espresso grounds, and it was perfect."

(141) Kali is the name of a Hindu goddess.

(142) Costume designer Kimberly Adams worked on season one. She looked at eighties school photo archives for inspiration. "Will is the youngest in the family. His mom doesn't have a lot of money. He would have had hand-me-downs... I really tried to get, same with his brother as well, just that kind of that odd, ill-fitting, not trendy-of-the-time kind of fit. Different than somebody like Mike, whose family was upper-middle class and conservative. He would have had newer things for the school year."

(143) On the character of Eleven, costume designer Kimberly Adams said this - "I loved working with Millie Bobby Brown! Not your typical 11 year old, an old soul! She brought so much to that character! I sketched out her looks to make sure we captured what the Duffers envisioned. The hospital gown had to be a clue where a piece of it is found later. Benny's t-shirt he puts her in had to be specific. When she had to get clothes from Mike's house, we tried her in his clothes and of course she was adorable! The dress that the boys find in the attic had to be special and something that would have been Nancy's that would have been saved. I tried various period girls dressed from the 70's to find the right shape, and we built multiples so it could carry over to being aged as the episodes progressed. Millie brought so much emotion to the character with virtually no words, like a silent star!"

(144) On the character of Barb, costume designer Kimberly Adams said this - "We had a blast finding her character, but I did not see that one coming! I'm so happy for Shannon [Purser] and so happy that she resonated with the audience! We had fun discovering her character in the fitting. I had laid

out her look in a board and gathered real period pieces but she evolved with the casting of Shannon. I believe it was Shannon's first role, so fittings were new to her, but she enjoyed the process of discovering the character. We tried lots of clothing, but when she put on that first ruffled plaid blouse, we both looked at each other and knew we had found her! Again, when you see the actor become the character in the mirror it's really rewarding!"

(145) For the Ghostbusters costumes in season two, costume designer Kim Wilcox said: "We thought about whose costume would be more 'together' and whose would be less, and whose mom maybe made it from scratch and whose mom didn't."

(146) Sadie Sink nearly lost the part of Max Mayfield because when they auditioned her because she was initially too tall compared to the other young actors on the show.

(147) Nearly a thousand boys were auditioned for the parts of Mike, Dustin, Lucas, and Will.

(148) Finn Wolfhard was one young cast member who didn't have to brush up on eighties movies. He'd already seen most of them.

(149) Before they became famous for Stranger Things, the Duffer Brothers worked for M. Night Shyamalan on the sci-fi horror mystery series Wayward Pines.

(150) Stranger Things was the acting debut of Shannon Purser.

(151) In the video arcade in Stranger Things 2 there is a game called Quest for the Space Knife. In reality there was no such game. It was a joke on behalf of the crew as one of them was in a band called Space Knife.

(152) The Duffer Brothers say that they don't like the game Dig Dug very much but felt it was a perfect title for one of the episodes featuring tunnels.

(153) David Harbour says Chester the dog was the most difficult actor to work with on the set! "The dog was the worst on the set. There was a day with this dog that was the worst actor I've ever worked with in my life. The dog was just being a jerk. I never — I walked off set. I've never done that before. There's footage of me like throwing a fit, going like, 'I'm gonna be in my trailer!' and just storming off. Cause the damn dog wouldn't do what it was supposed to do. It was just supposed to bark at a thing. And there was a trainer who was off camera yelling like, 'C'mon, we gotta make our money, this is how we make our money!' And I was like, 'this is weird.'"

(154) Caleb McLaughlin nearly didn't turn up for the Stranger Things auditions because he was dejected at the time after some rejections for other acting jobs.

(155) Millie Bobby Brown said at Asia Comic Con that the story that her father burst into tears when she had her hair shaved is false. She said her mother was the one who got upset at the thought of her long hair being cut.

(156) David Harbour said this about the origins of Hopper's hat - "Orlando Palacios at Worth & Worth designed that hat for me. He actually made a hat for me for the Black Mass premiere in Toronto. I fell in love with him and his shop, so much that I went back to him when we were developing the character of Hopper, and on paper, there was no hat for Hopper. So I told the Duffers that I wanted an iconic hat, like the pork pie in The French Connection, or Indy's fedora. I went to Orlando and said, "hey, this guy was born in 43, he's 40 years old in 1983, let's talk about a hat for him. Maybe he went to Vietnam, or maybe his dad was in World War II.". And Orlando says, "great, maybe it's his dad's hat. There's a

hat called the open road that Eisenhower used to wear.. So we developed this open road hat that was great, and we had three of them made for the character. Orlando is an extraordinary artist, and he's really detail-oriented, so if you look carefully at the hat, you'll see the remnants of a band, which is an invisible band – that's created when things are faded when the Sun hits them. So we decided that at one point it was his father's hat, and then the band fell off, but Hopper still wears it. That was really important to me, and I felt like it was something I could mess around with, and it felt like an old glove. But it also felt like something he could hide behind. In many ways, Hopper likes to hide and he doesn't want people to see the pain that he experiences every day and doesn't want people to see what he's feeling. So he has this big wide brim, a 3 inch rim that he can pull down and hide behind."

(157) The real shooting location for Hawkins High School is the Patrick Henry High School in Atlanta, Georgia.

(158) The shooting location for Hawkins Library is the Butts County Probate Court in Jackson, Georgia.

(159) Linnea Berthelsen, who plays Kali, was philosophical about the mixed reception of The Lost Sister episode which she featured in. "I haven't really paid much attention to it, it's not my storyline and I didn't write it, and I didn't direct it. I just admire the Duffers for taking big risks this season and I think it's really brave and really great that they're doing it."

(160) Millie Bobby Brown estimates that she only had to really eat the equivalent of two eggo waffles despite all the scenes of Eleven with them in season one.

(161) Noah Schnapp says it wasn't much fun shooting the scene in the finale of season one when will coughs up the slug.

"They made this weird mixture of... I think it was licorice and gummies and apple sauce. I actually thought it would taste good! So I took a big scoop on the first take, and I put it in the back of my mouth, and oh God, it was so disgusting. At the beginning of the scene, I'm supposed to pretend it's not in my mouth, and then I cough it up. But inside, I was already gagging."

(162) Steven Spielberg was responsible - as either a director or producer - for a remarkable number of films that are referenced in Stranger Things. They include Poltergeist. E.T, the Indiana Jones series, The Goonies, and Minority Report.

(163) In the finale of season two at the Snow Ball when Mike and Eleven dance, Finn Wolfhard can be seen whispering "I'm coming in" as a warning to Millie Bobby Brown that he's about to kiss her.

(164) The reunion of Mike and Eleven was originally going to occur at the Snow Ball dance but the Duffers decided to have them meet again at the end of the penultimate episode instead.

(165) Winona Ryder and Matthew Modine appeared together in the music video for Roy Orbison's A Love So Beautiful.

(166) When Millie Bobby Brown was in the sensory deprivation water tank in the Hawkins Lab, the Duffers communicated with her through a radio in her ear.

(167) The Duffers were initially reluctant to cast Sean Astin. They felt it was too much of a 'gimmick' because of his Goonies association. "They actually hesitated to hire me because I was in The Goonies," says Astin, "because the critical thing is you're not distracted. So one of the coolest things for me, for Bob, is coming into the Byers house and seeing these walls and the floor and the ceiling all taken over with Will's map."

(168) Natalia Dyer made her film debut in Hannah Montana: The Movie.

(169) The official posters for the first and second seasons were created by Kyle Lambert. They were designed to mimic eighties movie poster maestro Drew Struzan.

(170) Stranger Things was shot on a digital cinema camera. A layer of scanned film grain was added to the colouring process so that Stranger Things would look more like an eighties show.

(171) Jim Hopper is the name of the character that Arnold Schwarzenegger and his military team are looking for at the start of the 1987 film Predator.

(172) Hawkins is the name of the character Shane Black plays in Predator.

(173) David Harbour's new found fame has seen him take over the role of comic book hero Hellboy.

(174) The building used to depict the Hawkins Department of Energy is an abandoned mental institution in Atlanta.

(175) It was formerly Georgia Mental Health Institute but now Emory University Briarcliff Campus, 1256 Briarcliff Road, Atlanta.

(176) The Duffers say the former mental institution had tunnels underneath so that patients could be taken in without the public seeing them. The Duffers found this quite disturbing.

(177) The interior scenes for the laboratory are filmed in a studio.

(178) The quarry scenes were shot at Bellwood Quarry, Atlanta.

(179) The location for Will's 'funeral' in season one was Bethany Cemetery, Rivers Road, Fayetteville.

(180) Winona Ryder got through the tough season one shoot by eating a lot of veggie burgers.

(181) Shawn Levy directed some first season episodes to give the Duffers a 'breather'. It gave them more time to finish the scripts for the later episodes.

(182) Japanese anime helped inspire Stranger Things. Akira and Elfen Lied in particular.

(183) Dustin's sneakers in season one are K-Swiss Heaven S. Mike wears PUMAS and Lucas is fond of Saucony.

(184) As far as footwear goes, both Eleven and Millie Bobby Brown seem to like Converse.

(185) In season two, Steve Harrington eats Kentucky Fried Chicken at Barb's parents and comments that he loves "KFC". This was seen as a mistake or anachronism by some as Kentucky Fried Chicken had yet to rebrand themselves as KFC. However, others feel it wasn't a mistake and that "KFC" was already a common term used in 1984 by an unquantifiable number of people who frequented the fast food establishment.

(186) Dart was voiced by sound designer Craig Henighan.

(187) There is a mistake when Eleven levitates Mike's toy Millennium Falcon. The toy has clear engines at the back. The original Millennium Falcon toy had orange stickers to depict

the engines.

(188) According to the Hollywood Reporter, the child actors were paid $30,000 an episode in season one.

(189) Charlie Heaton says he won the part of Jonathan while conducting a Skype audition in a London burger bar! Heaton says the Duffers were looking for actors who were not well known and this worked to his advantage.

(190) There is a mistake when Eleven steals the eggos from the supermarket. The display near the entrance has Trident White chewing gum. This gum was only introduced in 2001.

(191) The woodland scenes in season one were shot at Georgia International Horse Park. This 1,400-acre park held all of the equestrian events for the 1996 Centennial Olympic Games.

(192) The real location exterior for the hospital in the finale of season one is East Point First Baptist Church at 2813 East Point St in East Point, Georgia.

(193) Joe Keery said he nearly hit Sadie Sink by accident with his (resin) baseball bat shooting the junkyard scene in Stranger Things 2.

(194) Dustin complains about Nilla Wafers not being real ones at the funeral of Will in season one. Nilla Wafers are wafer style cookies. They are often used in banana pudding recipes.

(195) The PEZ dispenser Dustin brings along with the food in his backpack to search for Will is a Jack in the Box clown. This is a mistake as it was made in 1999.

(196) The Byers house exterior in Stranger Things is a ramshackle house the production designers found near some woods in Georgia. The interior scenes in the Byers house are

all shot in a studio.

(197) The visual effects department said in interviews that one of the most difficult sequences to do was the scene in the finale where Eleven pins the Demogorgon to a blackboard and they both vanish in a cloud of dust.

(198) Millie Bobby Brown, who was living in London at the time, did her Skype audition with a fake but convincing American accent. This impressed the casting director.

(199) Shawn Levy says that virtually nothing is cut from Stranger Things as the Duffers whittle the material down until they think it is right. There would not be enough leftovers for any deleted scenes. "It's really, really interesting because in a given two-hour movie there's usually at least half an hour of scenes that get cut. On Stranger Things, both seasons, because the Duffers write and rewrite and rewrite they just like hammer this material so rigorously before it ever shoots that everything has a purpose. They also don't believe in scenes that aren't plot necessary. So you'll notice there's very few scenes — even like a delicious treat like Billy flirting with Karen Wheeler, it serves a purpose; he's trying to get information from her. So because the Duffers like all scenes to anchor into plot and necessity it means there's very, very, very few deleted scenes."

(200) As Levy says, The Duffers feel that every scene in Stranger Things serves the plot no matter how inconsequential it may seem. Every scene is there for an important reason.

(201) Rejected test designs for the Stranger Things titles logo include one based on the titles for Ridley Scott's Alien. In the end they went for the Stephen King paperback design.

(202) The Ghostbusters uniforms the boys wear were flight or mechanic suits adapted. Will's was the only that was made

from scratch (because they wanted it to look more homemade than the others).

(203) The Duffers say that they didn't really play Dungeons & Dragons as kids.

(204) Finn Wolfhard was cast because the Duffers liked the nervous energy he had.

(205) The Duffers say there were no alternatives to the child actors they cast. They felt they had found the only children capable of playing these parts.

(206) In season one, you can see a Dish Network satellite dish on a roof. These were not sold until 1994.

(207) Joe Keery hurt his back in the junkyard sequence in season two because he had to do so many takes of him jumping into the bus.

(208) Sadie Sink says it was slightly strange to act out scenes where she hates Billy because in real life she and Dacre Montgomery are good friends.

(209) Atlanta was chosen as the shooting location because the production team found that the surrounding areas had a very 'anytown' feel. With some modifications they could made to look very generic Americana.

(210) Georgia's competitive tax incentives for television and film probably helped too!

(211) The interiors of the Hawkins Lab were designed to look like a nightmarish cold war facility. The production designers wanted it to look like a place used to store secrets. It had to be cold and alienating.

(212) The real location for Hawkins Middle School is Patrick Henry Academy at 109 S. Lee St. in Stockbridge, Georgia.

(213) The movie theatre location in season one is at 2 N. Oak St. in Jackson. This isn't a real cinema. A furniture store was made to look like a cinema from the outside.

(214) The cinema in Hawkins is showing the Tom Cruise film All the Right Moves in season one.

(215) The real life Benny's Burgers is Tiffany's Kitchen, 7413 Lee Road, Lithia Springs.

(216) The gas station where Steve argues with his friends in season one was shot in Winston, GA on US 78. The gas station has since been demolished.

(217) Millie Bobby Brown and Sadie Sink became such good friends on the Stranger Things 2 set they went on a family vacation together.

(218) The second season had a budget of $8 million per episode.

(219) A deal was struck in 24 hours when Netflix were approached about the show.

(220) The Duffers killed off Benny and Barb because they wanted the audience to feel that none of the characters were safe.

(221) The show was pitched as an anthology early on but this idea was quickly abandoned.

(222) The games in the video arcade were all real and playable.

(223) Sadie Sink says that - unlike her character Max - in real life she was terrible at playing the video games in the arcade. The only one she even understood was Pac-Man.

(224) Millie Bobby Brown says she unwittingly slipped back into her natural English accent a few times while playing Eleven in the first season and had to be reminded to stay American.

(225) Noah Schnapp voiced Charlie Brown in The Peanuts Movie. Schnapp thinks that Charlie, unlike Will, wouldn't survive very long in the Upside Down!

(226) Movie posters we see on characters walls in season one include Jaws, The Thing, and The Evil Dead.

(227) In season one we briefly see some croquet mallets in the Byers house. This is an in-joke reference to the Winona Ryder film Heathers.

(228) In 2012, Caleb McLaughlin acted in The Lion King at the Minskoff Theatre. He played Simba.

(229) Millie Bobby Brown unsuccessfully auditioned for leading (child) roles in Logan and The BFG.

(230) Millie Bobby Brown is homeschooled and doesn't attend a school. She has this in common with Winona Ryder. Winona was homeschooled for some of her childhood.

(231) Hasbro released an Ouija board game based on the Christmas light scenes in season one.

(232) In season one, the cast members were only allowed to read one script at a time so they would have no idea of what would happen next.

(233) Holly Wheeler is dressed in very similar clothes to Drew Barrymore in E.T.

(234) Millie Bobby Brown felt sick shooting the finale of season two when Eleven closes the Gate because she and David Harbour were suspended on a platform that was swaying around.

(235) In 2015, the Duffers released a horror film they wrote and directed called Hidden. It has 53% on Rotten Tomatoes.

(236) The meat that Steve and Dustin use on the railway tracks and junkyard to attract Dart was in reality a mixture of watermelon and beef.

(237) Sadie Sink didn't enjoy the scenes with the beef and watermelon because she's a vegan.

(238) When the crow scares Hopper in the pumpkin field in Stranger Things 2 you can clearly detect a sample of the music from Predator.

(239) Millie Bobby Brown had no idea what a record player was when she was first introduced to eighties props.

(240) Millie Bobby Brown got a headache from all the epsom salt in the kiddie pool during the sensory deprivation scene.

(241) Stranger Things is similar to a 2010 Canadian science fiction film called Beyond the Black Rainbow. Beyond the Black Rainbow is set in a secret lab and features a young woman with special powers. It also has a synth score. Matt Duffer has admitted that he was aware of Beyond the Black Rainbow.

(242) The Duffers say that Paul Reiser is not a huge fan of science fiction in real life. "I just don't always watch 'em.

That's not what I'm drawn to. Aliens was a similar thing where, first of all, it was early in my career. I was just thrilled to be invited into a big flashy picture like that. But I also knew it was going to be great. I knew Jim Cameron's skill and I read the script and I went, "Wow this thing is fantastic." When you get invited to play out of your comfort zone in a different world, it's a great opportunity."

(243) Reiser says his children told him that Stranger Things was cool and that he should accept the offer to be a part of it. "Two days after the show dropped last year was when I heard about it. My very hip 16-year-old son had seen it and said, "Hey Dad, you gotta check out this new show." So when they called and said, "Do you know about this new show Stranger Things?" I said, "Of course I do, I have my pulse on the American culture." But I was fortunate my son hipped me to it. I met them literally that next day and they told me very vaguely what they had: "It's going to be a guy who comes off as a very nice guy when you meet him." And I said, "Uh huh, what happens?" and they said, "You'll see!""

(244) Unlike the Duffers, David Harbour says he played Dungeons & Dragons as a child.

(245) David Harbour says that as a young man he had hair just like Steve Harrington!

(246) Paul Reiser and Matthew Modine starred together in the 1995 film Bye Bye Love.

(247) Matthew Modine says that he doesn't personally remember much about the 1980s because he was too busy. Modine acted in a dozen films in that decade - including the gruelling Full Metal Jacket for Stanley Kubrick.

(248) In Stranger Things 2, you can hear a small burst of the music from Joe Dante's Gremlins when Dart escapes from the

AV room.

(249) Mr Clarke's analogy to the boys in season one concerning alternate dimensions is this - "Picture an acrobat standing on a tightrope. That's our dimension. And our dimension has rules. You can move forwards or backwards. But, what if, right next to our acrobat there is a flea. And the flea can also travel back and forth, just like our acrobat right? The flea can also travel this way, along the side of the rope. He can even go underneath the rope."

(250) Cosmologist Ranga-Ram Chary felt that Mr Clarke's analogy wasn't perfect. He suggested this alternative - "You are stuck in a traffic jam. You can only go forward, backward or change lanes. That is being stuck in two dimensions. If you could get the car to get off the ground (there are a few prototypes that I have seen), that would help you move in a third dimension. Strictly speaking even that isn't accurate, because the driver is extended in the third dimension. But then, neither is the flea or a tightrope — both of which are three-dimensional objects!"

(251) Nancy is disgusted in season one when Mike puts syrup on his scrambled eggs at breakfast. However, breakfast recipes involving scrambled eggs and syrup are far from uncommon!

(252) When Joyce has a flashback to happier times with Will at his Castle Byers den in the woods, she has tickets to see the 1982 Tobe Hopper/Steven Spielberg film Poltergeist. Poltergeist was originally rated R but Spielberg successfully lobbied for it to be a PG.

(253) In season two, when he gives Nancy and Jonathan a tour of the lab, Dr Owens quotes George Sarton. George Sarton (1884 – 1956) was a Belgian-American chemist and science historian.

(254) Of the five main kids in season one, Caleb McLaughlin is the oldest (born October 13, 2001) and Noah Schnapp the youngest (born October 3, 2004).

(255) Charlie Heaton says he identifies with the character of Jonathan because his own background is quite modest and his family was far from rich.

(256) Matt Duffer says that Matthew Modine had to figure out the character of Brenner as he was rather vague in the early script. "When we cut to him as little as we do and give him so little dialogue, how do you make him an interesting character? That's a character who we didn't really figure out until we started working with Matthew. And he brought a lot himself. He informed it, and I'm really happy with where we wound up with him at the end, with something that was discovered during the course of shooting, really."

(257) Barb has a Trapper Keeper folder in season one. Trapper Keeper is a brand of loose-leaf binder created by Mead. Popular with students from the 1970s to the 1990s, it featured sliding plastic rings, folders, and pockets to keep schoolwork and papers in.

(258) The Puffer Vest coat of Will Byers in season one mimics the one worn by Michael J Fox in Back to the Future.

(259) Craig Henighan created the sound effects for when Holly Wheeler walks towards the Christmas lights in season one.

"For most of the electrical sounds, I recorded little electric things around my house, and things I had in my garage. I don't ever throw out old electric things that make noise. I keep bins of old toothbrushes, shavers, phones, etc. The one main thing I used was my battery charger, which has a 50 amp setting on it. I recorded that and then took little pieces, to which I added light bulb filament sounds. I broke some light bulbs and Christmas lights and I recorded the sound that the filament makes when you shake it a little bit. Of course, these are such low-level sounds – so I had to crank the heck out of them just to get them at a volume that I could use. So that was the two core sounds and then the other main thing I wanted to do, either when Joyce or the little girl was following the light bulbs, was actually have a little tone play. So I found a little tone in a synth patch and I used it for a little touch. I used Close Encounters as an idea of how to make somebody follow something in a simple sort of way. Those are the three main elements and I manipulated those using pitching and stretching, to make them feel similar but different enough, to give you a breadcrumb trail of sounds to follow. Particularly for the little girl, I wanted the sound to start small and then build up when she gets into the bedroom and the lights flicker all around her."

(260) Sean Astin auditioned for the part of Murray Bauman. He ended up playing Bob Newby.

(261) The extras hired for the Snow Ball scenes were not told at first that they had been hired for Stranger Things. They soon worked it out though.

(262) David Harbour said this of acting in the Upside Down scenes - "In the show it's amazing and beautiful, but on the actual set, it's really silly. There's a bunch of purple piping that looks really fake and it pulsates, so it kind of feels like you're in a haunted house. For the spores, there's a dude with a big 'ol pillowcase full of dandelions and a big fan. So you're walking down the hall and then this guy is just standing there blowing dandelions at you."

(263) The goo in Shannon Purser's mouth when Barb is found dead in the Upside Down is made of baby food, olive oil,

water, and some marmalade.

(264) Charlie Heaton found it hard to say the word Nancy in an American accent and kept sounding British so he was dubbed whenever he said Nancy's name in the show.

(265) Twenty tons of ice were needed to make Georgia look like Hawkins in winter.

(266) Bob's death in Stranger Things 2 is a homage to the demise of shark hunter Quint in Jaws.

(267) Mark Steger was given a two month development period to get used to the Demogorgon suit.

(268) Gaten Matarazzo, Caleb McLaughlin and Sadie Sink knew each other before Stranger Things from working in shows on Broadway.

(269) There are a number of Indiana Jones and the Temple of Doom references in Stranger Things 2. The thugee cult in the film worship the goddess Kali, Short Round can't reach the car pedals (just like Max), and Indy and Willie's flirting in the palace is homaged by Nancy and Jonathan at Murray's house.

(270) There are some anachronistic songs in Stranger Things. We hear There Is a Light That Never Goes Out by The Smiths at one point but this song wasn't recorded until 1985.

(271) Peyton Wich says it was difficult playing the odious bully Troy because the kids were so nice. "Troy was a hard character to play. All of the kids were so nice and amazing to work with not to mention we cut up… a lot. So, that being said, it was extremely difficult to be mean to these awesome people. I just had to mentally prepare for it."

(272) Peyton says the scene where Troy pees himself in the

school hall was quite embarrassing to shoot. And just for the record, he didn't really have to pee himself!

(273) The speech Nancy gives to Dustin when she dances with him at the Snow Ball is based on a similar pep talk a female cousin gave Ross Duffer when he was a kid.

(274) Millie Bobby Brown says she never googles herself and that her family run her social media accounts.

(275) When Nancy stabs the possessed Will with the poker in Stranger Things 2, they used the dummy of Will from season one where Hopper cuts into his body and finds it stuffed with cotton wool.

(276) Gaten Matarazzo says that, like Dustin, he would have 3 Musketeers in his top 3 candy bars.

(277) Randy Havens says, because of his role as Mr Clarke, he is always being asked science questions that he can't answer.

(278) Joe Keery auditioned for the part of Jonathan Byers. "Originally, I auditioned for Jonathan. They were having everybody across the country audition for that. And when I got the script, Steve was definitely a little harsher. He was having this party—I think it was on a beach, because it originally took place in Montauk, Long Island. And he was a total, total dick. He forced himself on Nancy. Way harsher. But I think the Duffer Brothers were up for incorporating ideas we would have into the characters, and I had an instant idea what Steve would be like. I based it on people in my life, and characters that you see in those movies. In my mind, I think he has qualities that make him sort of a jerk. And aloof. And maybe not the most intelligent guy. But at the end of the day, I think he really does mean well."

(279) David Harbour says he was worried that the

Hopper/Eleven cabin scenes might have a 'serial killer vibe'.
"I was terrified that the audience's takeaway would be that
this was either sexualized in some way or that it was in some
way dangerous. I was very, very proud and overwhelmed by
the response of people just getting that Hopper is a good guy
and that he does really love her and care about her and is
worried about her and that that relationship really resonated
on a father-daughter level."

(280) Shawn Levy gave away the fate of Bob at Comic Con
when he said Bob was the new Barb.

(281) When Mrs Wheeler is reading the romantic novel in the
bath in Stranger Things 2, the male character of the two lovers
on the cover is made to look like Billy.

(282) Dacre Montgomery improvised the moment where Billy
helps himself to a cookie while flirting with Mrs Wheeler in
the kitchen.

(283) In the school scenes where Dart is loose, the kids had to
act with a rubber model.

(284) The kids called the rubber Dart model 'sushi' on the set.

(285) Millie Bobby Brown has displayed her penchant for
rapping twice on the Jimmy Fallon show.

(286) Dustin and Will reference the comic X-Men-134 in
episode one. This is the Dark Phoenix storyline - one of the
inspirations for Eleven.

(287) Finn Wolfhard, when Mike sees Dustin's hair at the
Snow Ball, has an identical line that he says in the movie IT.
"Holy s***, what happened to you?"

(288) HP Lovecraft was an inspiration for Stranger Things.

Lovecraft was a horror author who imagined a universe full of inexplicable creatures, dimensions and entities that can't be explained.

(289) The Duffers say they have a 30 page document about the Upside Down they wrote to draw from.

(290) Joe Chrest, who plays Ted Wheeler, also teaches acting. "A lot of acting training is so 'me, me, me,' and how can I express myself, and I think that's the wrong approach. Knowing your role is more important. The creativity is in us naturally. We have it as children, and we lose it at some point because someone tells us that's not cool anymore. I'm teaching college students how to play kids' games. Because acting is more about imagination than knowledge and research. And I think this is what applies to any creative field or business: You have to tear away all of those barriers, the adult blinders we put on, and tap into free creative thought."

(291) In Stranger Things 2, Mike says he called Eleven every night for 353 days. 3 + 5 + 3 = 11.

(292) In season two, Dustin wears a Science Museum of Minnesota dinosaur hoodie. The museum made some new ones as a tribute but they were so popular the museum website crashed because of the demand.

(293) In episode four of season one, producer/director Shawn Levy has a cameo as the coroner.

(294) Hopper is drinking Schlitz beer when we are first introduced to him waking up in the morning.

(295) Hopper reads Eleven Anne of Green Gables in the cabin. He also is shown reading this to his daughter Sara in the season one finale.

(296) MK-Ultra plays a big part in the plot of Stranger Things. 'MK-Ultra was a top-secret CIA project in which the agency conducted hundreds of clandestine experiments — sometimes on unwitting U.S. citizens — to assess the potential use of LSD and other drugs for mind control, information gathering and psychological torture. Though Project MK-Ultra lasted from 1953 until about 1973, details of the illicit program didn't become public until 1975, during a congressional investigation into widespread illegal CIA activities within the United States and around the world.'

(297) Noah Schnapp has a twin sister in real life.

(298) Shawn Levy said that a bigger role was planned for Karen Wheeler in season two but they didn't have room for it in the end.

(299) Cara Buono says she would love a bigger role for Karen. "I think [the Duffer brothers] have been talking about tapping into really who she is. Is she more than just the 'happy' homemaker? Why is she married to Ted? There's not a lot there. The tension is just there in the writing. We are kind of that married couple where if you're married for a while there all those little arguments and little things that get to you. That's kind of where they are."

(300) Millie Bobby Brown and Randy Havens both signed up to appear in the 2019 movie Godzilla: King of the Monsters.

(301) Will Chase, who plays Billy's stern father, is a singer and actor known for his work on Broadway.

(302) In Stranger Things 2, the cinema is promoting The Terminator. We also see Eleven watching a Terminator trailer on television.

(303) When Jonathan rents movies from the video store for

Halloween in Stranger Things 2 he chooses Mr Mom, Wargames, and Twilight Zone: The Movie. Bob picks Mr Mom to watch.

(304) Millie Bobby Brown says she hates strawberry ice cream. She had to eat it though when Benny feeds her at the diner. They chose strawberry because it looked better on camera than vanilla.

(305) The makeup artist put sunburn glazing gel on Millie Bobby Brown for the scenes where Eleven is living in the woods because it made her look cold and frosted.

(306) David Harbour says that the biggest mystery about season two for him is how Hopper apparently managed to do such a professional job with Eleven's hair and make-up for the Snow Ball dance!

(307) Will tells Mike that the Upside Down visions are like being caught between View-Master slides. View-Master is the trademark name of a line of special-format stereoscopes and corresponding View-Master "reels", which are thin cardboard disks containing seven stereoscopic 3-D pairs of small colour photographs on film. In the 1980s, many kids had View-Masters and they often had film tie-in slides to view.

(308) The Lost Sister episode features graffiti that references Grant Morrison's comic The Invisibles.

(309) The sequence is Stranger Things 2 where Will is tied down and subjected to questions is inspired by John Carpenter's The Thing.

(310) The Duffers asked that the acne and blemishes of the children not be completely covered by the makeup department because they wanted them to look like ordinary kids.

(311) Finn Wolfhard considers himself to be something of a doughnut connoisseur.

(312) The handgun used by the military personal at the Hawkins Lab in season one is the Beretta 92FS.

(313) Connie Frazier uses a Colt M1911A1.

(314) Chief Hopper seems to use a Smith & Wesson Model 66.

(315) The government agents also use the Heckler & Koch MP5K submachine gun.

(316) In season two, Hopper has a Colt Python.

(317) Hopper has a Colt Model 723 M16A2 Carbine in the last few episodes.

(318) Hopper also has an Ithaca 37 shotgun in the finale.

(319) When Will is threatened in the shed in episode one of Stranger Things he picks up a Mossberg 144 LS rifle.

(320) Title sequence designer Eric Demeusy said a lot of thought went into the Stranger Things titles. "In this case because of the time period of the show and the thriller aspect to it there was an intention to throw it back to classic 80's thriller book covers. Originally the logo had pointed serifs which added a bit of menace to the lettering but was later changed out. I tend to think of serif to be more classic. I think it's just a matter of trying to change it up. The logo stayed pretty true to what was in the design boards from the beginning. The only real change was a slightly different modified typeface. We went through many versions of the sequence when it came to which letters we see in each shot and what parts of the letters we see. We experimented with

having the sequence be one long zoom out as well. Overall it was a very fun process and everyone on board loved the direction we were going."

(321) Charlie Heaton was starstruck working with Winona Ryder. "I mean, she is an icon and she's worked with some of the best people. Yeah, I freaked out a little on the inside, but I tried to keep it together. She's gorgeous and cool. It was nice, we hit it off pretty well. It was just super fun to be able to hang out with her. She gave me some t-shirts, actually, as presents."

(322) Sadie Sink had to wear fake tan because Max is supposed to be from California. "Yeah, they wanted my character to be this California girl that spends a lot of time in the sun, and I don't look like I spend a lot of time in the sun because I don't - sun is my worst enemy. So they wanted to give me a subtle sun-kissed glow, so they put some tanner on my face and on my hands. I just remember the smell being so distinct, so when I think of my experience on Stranger Things I think of that smell."

(323) Sadie Sink says she was overwhelmed when she learned she'd won the part of Max. "I was at school at my speaking debate practice and my mom texted me and was like, "Get in the car right now." I was like, "Mom, I can't, I have to practice!" and she was like, "No I don't care you need to get in the car." So I knew something was off. I was like, "Why do you need me in the car so fast?" and she said, "I need to take your sister to a play date!" and I was really confused. So then I started to put everything together and realized that I must have been getting a call from the director soon to tell me I got the part. Sure enough, when I got home the phone rang and my mom handed it to me and they told me I got it. I didn't really know how to process it. I just stood there stunned. I think there's a video of me or picture of me somewhere and I'm just on the phone and my face was so shocked and I

couldn't stop smiling."

(324) Kyle Dixon says he and Michael Stein were brought in to work on the score for Stranger Things right from the very start. "The very beginning. The first thing we saw was the trailer they made with our song in it before they shot anything. We saw a little look-book with inspiration, synopsis, character stuff, we saw scripts before they had even done any casting. We were doing demos for themes prior to casting. They actually used some of the demos against the auditions to help decide, I guess, both on the music and who they would get to act in it. So we were involved from the very beginning, I would say. Not the very beginning but early on. They had only written maybe two or three episodes when we came on. They definitely wanted the music to be a big part of it and that's why they brought us in so early. So we worked on it for a fairly substantial amount of time because they wanted to make sure it was right which was good for us because we were just learning the ropes on scoring. It definitely helped us figure out what we were doing."

(325) Millie Bobby Brown has two sisters and an older brother named Charlie Brown.

(326) What are Kyle Dixon's most beloved eighties movie scores? "I don't know. I don't know if it's my favourite film but The Keep by Michael Mann has a great score, a Tangerine Dreams score. That's a really good score and the movie is cool too. Sorcerer, another Tangerine Dreams score that's really good, not very similar to Stranger Things necessarily. Those two are Tangerine Dreams, I don't want everything to be Tangerine Dreams. I don't know. So many good scores. Stalker is one of my favourites, and also has a wonderful score by Edward Artemyev."

(327) Caleb McLaughlin says aspiring actors must learn to cope with rejection. "You're going to get rejected a lot. I still

will get rejected. You just [need to] grow a thicker skin. And I think [you should] do community theater, watch movies [with] your favorite actors, and just work on your craft, and one day, you'll nail a job. It took me a while to get where I am now. What people really think is it happened overnight—it didn't. It took a few years and discipline. It happened quicker with my positive energy. You can't always think negative; I always thought, I'm gonna get that. Your competition is yourself. Don't think about anyone else because when you think about someone else, you go to the other track, and that's not yours."

(328) Caleb McLaughlin says that when people told him they didn't like his character (presumably because Lucas is mean to Eleven) in season one he took that as a compliment because it meant he had played his part well.

(329) Shawn Levy says auditioning children is very different to auditioning adult actors. "I'm looking for not only talent, but that special synchronicity between the actor and the character. So, with the kids on our show, we definitely talk with them more before and after their reading than we do with most adults auditioning. With an adult actor, you're betting so much on the reading. With a kid actor, you're betting just as much on their innate quality in real life in the room. I can tell you for a fact we saw 1,000 kids [for] Stranger Things, and many, many talented kids didn't get the part. I always tell my actor friends, you can nail an audition and you can be incredibly talented, and sometimes you still won't get the part if it's not in sync with the filmmakers' vision of that character and their feeling—or lack of feeling)—that that person is in the room with them. So much of it comes down to that stuff beyond an actor's control. That's important to remember so you don't beat yourself up for the wrong reasons."

(330) In 2017 Netflix closed down a Stranger Things pop up

bar in Chicago - but in the nicest way possible. Esquire: 'A few months back, Emporium Popups opened the Upside-Down in Chicago, a Stranger Things-themed bar that served Eggo-inspired cocktails under Winona Ryder's crazy twinkle lights. It was a hit among fans, who packed the place to drink booze amongst set pieces that looked pretty damn close to the real deal. But, like all good things that have the potential to divert profits and creative direction from giant corporations into independent enterprises, the pop-up is coming to an end. Netflix sent a letter to the owners of Emporium Popups firmly telling them that the Upside Down must close. The letter itself, however, written by a very dedicated and enthusiastically nerdy lawyer, doesn't disappoint. Read for yourself, per DNAinfo...'

'My walkie-talkie is busted so I had to write this note instead. I heard you launched a Stranger Things pop-up bar at your Logan Square location. Look, I don't want you to think I'm a total wastoid, and I love how much you guys love the show. (Just wait until you see Season 2!) But unless I'm living in the Upside Down, I don't think we did a deal with you for this pop-up. You're obviously creative types, so I'm sure you can appreciate that it's important to us to have a say in how our fans encounter the worlds we build. We're not going to go full Dr Brenner on you, but we ask that you please (1) not extend the pop-up beyond its 6 week run ending in September, and (2) reach out to us for permission if you plan to do something like this again. Let me know as soon as possible that you agree to these requests. We love our fans more than anything, but you should know that the demogorgon is not always as forgiving. So please don't make us call your mom.'

(331) When Kali and Eleven target Ray Carroll, the lab worker who mistreated Eleven's mother Terry Ives, Carroll is watching Punky Brewster. Punky Brewster was a sitcom for younger viewers about an orphan girl adopted by a cranky but kind hearted man.

(332) Finn Wolfhard fired his agent Tyler Grasham, after at least two accusations of sexual assault were made against Grasham.

(333) David Harbour loved the character of Hopper from the moment he read the script. "When I read the character, it reminded me a lot of Roy Scheider from Jaws. It reminded me a lot of Nick Nolte in those old 48 Hours movies. It reminded me a little bit of Indiana Jones. It just reminded me of all these leading men that I had grown up with as a child when I went to movies in the '80s. I hadn't seen a character, at least one has not really come across my radar, that is so messy in a certain way and so complex. I just sort of fell in love with him. I like the whole story, too. I thought it was great, but in general, I really just fell in love with him."

(334) David Harbour said he was slightly suspicious that Netflix were trying to 'bury' the show before it came out. Luckily, this turned out be a false alarm. "It was so funny, because of Netflix's marketing — and I don't know if this was conscious or not, because I know they liked the show, but I don't know if they even knew it was going to be a hit — a couple weeks before the show started to air, there were no posters. I live in New York City, and there were no posters on buses, there was no advertising going on."

(335) David Harbour described the approach to the second season this way - "You have a very successful show, and then people want you to kind of come out and do the same thing. It's like having a hit song or something. People just want you to sing the hit song over and over again. In a way, you create kind of vanilla ice cream for the first season. Everybody's like, 'Holy s***, vanilla ice cream's so good.' For the second season, I think there's this feeling where you're like you don't want to do vanilla. You want to do strawberry ice cream. I think people will feel like maybe they like vanilla ice cream better

than they like strawberry ice cream, but we're going to create the best strawberry ice cream we can. We don't want to recreate vanilla."

(336) Joe Keery says he loved the Steve/Dustin team up and shooting the 'Farrah Fawcett' scene. "That was one of my favorite scenes to film. What I really like about that scene is you see Steve for the first time let his guard down with this kid. The characters kind of come together because they're both kind of left in the dust. They find what they need in each other. It ends up helping both of them and they learn from it. That scene is a moment where they both let their guard down and you can see that he really cares about this kid, and it's helpful in his journey to care more about others than he does himself. It's also these two characters who think they have it all figured out—but in no way have it all figured out. Also, Gaten is such a genius; he's such a smart funny kid. And I'm learning so many things about how to be spontaneous and relaxing. I'm ready to get back to work and shoot more. The kid is obviously 10 years younger than me, but he feels more mature than me. He's a gracious kid, man; he has a really good head on his shoulders. A lot of people ask me how the kids are, and the kids are doing excellent. They're dealing with such a crazy thing going on in their life."

(337) Natalia Dyer says she knew very quickly that the show was becoming a pop culture phenomenon. "I was very nervous as to how it would be received, but literally the first night that it came out, I got recognized on the street—I was living in New York at the time, so you're on the street a lot. To see that amping up, people recognizing you everywhere, and just seeing face to face how people felt about the show and how much it meant to them, it was wild! When people approach me, it's a vulnerable moment for everybody. You can see that sometimes people don't quite know what to say to you, but they want to come up to you and you can tell they're nervous, and it's really humbling and endearing. Generally

the message is just appreciation, people saying how much they love the show. It's wild and hard to wrap your mind around, but it's always been positive feedback, so it's the most you could hope for!"

(338) Winona Ryder says her casting in Stranger Things was quite mundane and simple. "Um, gosh, I wish I had a more interesting or exciting story. But I was sent the script and I'd had one experience in television, a HBO miniseries called Show Me a Hero. I had a small part, but I really wanted to work with David Simon. But I really didn't know much about the world of television; I just knew that it was becoming incredibly interesting and much more like film than films. But you know, I met with them (the Duffers). I really only was given a script of the pilot episode. We had a good meeting and I sort of took the leap. It's been sort of overwhelming with the reaction. I don't think any of us were prepared, but it's been really amazing. To work with the really incredibly talented young actors has been great."

(339) Millie Bobby Brown wasn't allowed to say to anyone she would back in season two when it started production so that Eleven's return would be more of a surprise when the promotion started.

(340) Shannon Purser says she loves the Barb Stranger Things fan art she has seen. "It's been totally surreal. I love it! The fan art is definitely one of my favourite things that have come up from the show. I'm an artist, I draw a bit, and I just love creativity and all forms of art. I love that people were inspired by the show and the characters and just inspired to create. I think that's what good art does. It breeds more creativity. I can't even explain how crazy it feels to have your own face being drawn over and over. It's absolutely incredible."

(341) Production designer Chris Trujillo says a crucial part of his job on Stranger Things is "fastidious estate sale pillaging.

Every weekend in the suburbs outside big cities there are time capsules being opened up for the discerning decorator to dig through. One dead man's junk drawer is another man's period perfect set dressing."

(342) Shawn Levy says it isn't really a proper season of Stranger Things if Joyce's house doesn't get trashed by monsters!

(343) The man who designed ITC Benguiat font used in Stranger Things' title sequence and those old Stephen King covers is Ed Benguiat. A British newspaper contacted the then 88 year-old Benguiat to ask him about the title sequence and found that Benguiat had never actually heard of Stranger Things. He describes the font he designed this way - "It merges, it moves in and out, it's very good. It's rather pleasing and comfortable too. And yet exciting at the same time. It's rather appropriate, if I might say. It lends itself to the feeling of the titles, it has a look. It's like food – it's hard to describe what something tastes like, or identify a good smell."

(344) The sketches that Will draws in Stranger Things 2 (which eventually cover most of the Byers) house were mostly done by scenic artists but Noah Schnapp personally contributed many himself!

(345) When Eleven is watching television alone in Hopper's cabin in Stranger Things 2 the actress she impersonates is Susan Lucci in All My Children.

(346) When we see the Wheeler family eating with Dustin as a guest, they are having meatloaf, mashed potato and green beans.

(347) Millie Bobby Brown says that when she bumped into Caleb McLaughlin again for the first time after having her hair shaved for the part of Eleven he had no idea who she was at

first.

(348) In Stranger Things 2, Hopper makes Eleven a Triple-Decker Eggo Extravaganza and jokes that the good thing is that it's only 8,000 calories. It looked like Hopper had added whipped cream, Reese's Pieces, Hershey's Kisses, and jelly beans to the stack.

(349) Matt Duffer said he was worried that, because there are so many television shows out there, that Stranger Things might have got lost in the crowd. "There's so much content out there in the world that the fear was you're just going to get lost. Even if people do like it, and we thought best case scenario is we're appealing to people like us who are nostalgic for this style of storytelling. So the surprise to us came when especially the younger generation started to fall in love with these characters, and then start tweeting about it and then word started to spread. Netflix was always behind the show and they always loved it. ... What they told us is that they were hoping that word of mouth would spread, but it's going to take some time. Word of mouth is certainly what got the show its popularity, but I think everyone was taken aback by how quickly that word of mouth spread."

(350) Millie Bobby Brown is friends with Maddie Ziegler. Ziegler is famous as the child dancing in music videos by Sia.

(351) Matty Cardarople, who plays the cheese puff loving arcade manager Keith, had a spit bucket so he wouldn't have to eat too many Cheetos.

(352) Noah Schnapp says it was difficult to shoot the sequence where Will is attacked by the Smoke Monster in the field. "That was such a hard scene to film. When they filmed the scene, there's nothing there, they're not gonna put a fake monster in the sky. So it was just a big green screen and I had to imagine that there's this big terrifying monster coming after

me, and it was so hard to wrap my mind around that, so I had to imagine that. This was Will's moment in the season to stand up for himself and be courageous and this is not like Will. Will's usually the quiet kid. He doesn't talk too much and in this scene he's standing up for himself and it was a big scene for Will and for me as well, so I definitely had to prepare for it a lot. I did a lot of research on stories about kids getting possessed and stuff and things about that. I thought, "If he's taking me over, he's coming in my mind so I have to think about what it feels like." It was hard. I had to make it up a little by myself and I thought about what it feels like."

(353) Sound designer Craig Henighan uses Stutter Edit ('It's an effect. It's an instrument. It's Stutter Edit — an innovative tool for both studio and stage...') on Stranger Things. "During the sound design process, I used iZotope's Stutter Edit plug-in quite a bit. Stutter Edit is an effects plug-in that can manipulate an audio source in a multitude of ways. It works by constantly sampling the incoming audio and storing it in a buffer so that it can be used for repeating short loops or creating jagged cuts. This is a plug-in that I hadn't used much prior to this project, not because I didn't like it, but because I never really needed to dive into the capabilities it offered until working on this particular series."

(354) Bellwood Quarry, in addition to Stranger things, has also been used in The Walking Dead and The Hunger Games: Mockingjay Part 1.

(355) When Finn Wolfhard was slated by some fans when he seemed to ignore their requests for an autograph, he was defended by Game of Thrones star Sophie Turner on Twitter. "Damn, seeing fully grown adults wait outside the Stranger Things kids' hotels etc , and then abuse them when they don't stop for them is super weird. What adult in their right mind waits for a CHILD outside their hotel and B is then is offended when the CHILD doesn't stop. It doesn't matter if they are an

actor, they are kids first. Give them the space they need in order to grow without feeling like they owe anyone anything for living their childhood dreams."

(356) Millie Bobby Brown says she was mistaken for a boy a few times when she had her buzzcut. She said she used to tell people her name was Jon.

(357) The most emotional scene for Noah Schnapp to film was the one where Will tries to explain to Joyce what happened when the Mind Flayer seemed to assault him. "I had a few big challenges this season. There's a few. The first is the scene that I had to do probably with Winona, I think it was Episode 3, where I was talking to her about what I saw in the field and it was really emotional. And before that I'd never really done a scene like that. So when I heard the scene was coming up I was really nervous because I didn't know what to expect or how to bring out those emotions so I remember texting Winona [Ryder], 'cause I know she's done that all in Season 1 and I asked her, "How do you do it? I need advice!" I remember asking Sean Astin, too, and they both told me not to push it. "If it doesn't come don't force it." They also told me you really have to put yourself in a really emotional state to access those emotions so I made myself really let go and relaxed and not tense and it was very easy for me to be able to cry in that scene and feel what Will was feeling, so I put myself in his shoes. And then I just thought, "What would it feel like to be telling your mom about a night like that?" It was a hard scene to film and I remember the first few takes we were doing, they were good takes but they weren't great and I remember on the fifth or sixth take we were in the middle of the scene and Shawn Levy, who was directing the scene, he saw me building up my emotion and he knew that I could get it in the next take so we restarted the scene and we did it all in that next take and the whole scene was from that one take and it was prefect. It was probably also my most favourite scene to film 'cause I felt so proud of it and good about that scene after

I finished it. Also very relieved."

(358) David Harbour says he was worried about a 'sophomore slump' in season two. "I've gotta say, I've talked to different people in the production and the cast, and they're a lot more nervous. I was much more nervous for Season 2. Season 2, to me, is the big sophomore slump hurdle. I loved True Detective so much in Season 1, and then when the Season 2 monstrosity came around, I was like, "What is this show?! What have you done to this show?!" For me, the big hurdle is having this lightning in a bottle moment, where the stars aligned and you created a beautiful, amazing show that people loved, and can you do it again? Once you do it a second time, it's smooth sailing from then on out. I'm not nervous. I'm in the minority of that, though. There are other people – and I won't name names – who are like, "The fans can turn on you! Look at what they're doing with Star Wars!" Apparently, they're upset about Star Wars. I just trust these guys. The idea is to do four or five seasons, the Duffers have said, and I feel like, if we can do Season 2, we can do 3, 4 and 5 with no sweat. Right now, the world is so open. Hopper, at the end of two, kind of adopts Eleven, and the Upside Down still exists, even though we closed the gate. There's just so much story there, with the tension with Joyce, his adopting of Eleven, and his relationship with all the kids, even the teens, and then you have all of these backstories. He went to Vietnam, and we haven't gotten into that, at all. In the '60s, he was in Vietnam, and then he went to New York and was a cop there for a while, around the time of Frank Serpico. The tapestry is just so huge and wide and beautiful. Even the shit with his daughter and the death of Sara, there's so many secrets there. I felt like they had to prove that we could do it again and open up the world, but once you open up the world, it's a buffet, going forward. I see it as an open buffet, as opposed to a burden. We can feed you guys so many wonderful things. We can now feed you so much stuff 'cause we opened the world."

(359) Sadie Sink says she was too scared to watch season one and covered her eyes a lot of the time when she tried to view it.

(360) In an interview, the Duffers said that out of the first season episodes they like The Bathtub the most. "We feel a lot of affection for this episode, because it's a little bit bonkers. And, at least for us, it's the most purely fun episode of the season. Our three disparate story lines collide as our teens, kids, and adults all finally team up. After spending six hours trying to keep these story lines separate, it was incredibly satisfying to merge them into into one. At last, we could explore new dynamics. Eleven and Joyce, Dustin and Hopper, Nancy and Eleven ("Is that my dress?" is a favourite line of ours). If anything, this episode is also just a showcase for our three wonderful boys: Finn (Mike), Caleb (Lucas), and Gaten (Dustin). They really grew as actors over the course of the season, and we love them in this episode. But it wasn't easy to get there. We were several months into shooting at this point, and their nervousness had at this point all but totally evaporated."

(361) How did sound designer Craig Henighan go about creating the sound of the Demogorgon? "For every project that I do, I try to apply a set of rules for myself. Sometimes I stick to them and sometimes I throw them out after a little while! I didn't want to go down the normal animal route, using pigs or cats. I think in Alien they used cappuccino makers and peacocks amongst other sounds. So I try to be aware of those sounds and initially I thought I'd try not to make the Entity out of real animals or human sounds. I thought I could do it with dry ice and squeaks and other oddball sounds that I could record or that I've collected over the years. But, that sort of failed. A lot of those things just didn't sound right for this monster. I recorded my own voice and tried to manipulate that. I did a little bit early on with Dehumaniser (vocal processing software by Krotos, Ltd.) and other plug-ins to get

something working but that sounded a little too heavy-handed. I wanted to come up with something similar to Predator, in terms of having an identifiable vocal, because initially you don't see the Entity. I wanted it to sonically evoke creepiness and intellect. In all of my recordings, I didn't quite find what I wanted, but then I started looking through my libraries. I have to give credit to Tim Prebble, who runs Hiss and Roar out of New Zealand. It's a great boutique sound design/sound effects library. Years ago I bought his seal recordings, and in there I heard a few things that I felt I could use as the hook. I took that seal vocal, and tried to pitch it and mask it, and put a lot of sounds in there so that people wouldn't really know where it came from. But then I went back to pitching the seal vocals just a little bit, and shortening the length of it. In a cool kind of way, it's really simple and effective, and to the point. That's the core sound of the Entity. When we get into the flesh, I recorded splatty sounds of water hitting flour, and other splats. I also used some great stuff from Boom Library and my good friend Rob Nokes has done a lot of specific recordings for me over the years. I had other fleshy movement sounds and door squeaks, rubber yoga ball creaks. I did some dry ice recordings that are part of the Entity's bigger roars and screams."

(362) Paul Reiser said he liked the ambiguous nature of Dr Owens right from the start. "They told me who I was playing and they told me what they had in mind. It was sort of nebulous — is he a good guy or a bad guy? To be honest, I've only read a few of the scripts so I still don't know and I'm not sure they know. I think part of what they were tickled by was, to whatever extent people know me from Aliens, they're automatically going, "Oh this guy is no good." I don't know where they're going with it but it's a fun thing to play."

(363) In Stranger Things 2, Mr Clarke has a periodic table on his classroom wall containing elements that hadn't been discovered in 1984.

(364) Kyle Lambert says he was especially overwhelmed by the response to his Stranger Things 2 poster. "The recent work I did on Stranger Things 2 has been the most satisfying by far. I received such positive feedback about the season 1 art, that there was a built in expectation that the second poster needed to take things to the next level As I was working on the piece, I could sense the anticipation grow around the release of the show and it was impossible not to feel that pressure. This resulted in a very powerful feeling of relief once the art had been released around the world and fans expressed how much they loved it. My friends kept sending me photos of billboards in New York and London, and I was able to drive around L.A. to see the art in the places I visited when I was a kid - It really doesn't get any better than that."

(365) In the real eighties Dig Dug arcade game, you could only enter three digits for your high score. So Max wouldn't really have been able to type MADMAX.

(366) The elastic walls in the Byers house as will seems to reach out to Joyce from the Upside Down have many possible sources of inspiration. The television scenes in Poltergeist and the undulating walls in A Nightmare On Elm Street are the most obvious.

(367) Although Mike Wheeler has a poster for John Carpenter's The Thing it seems unlikely that he would have actually watched this R-rated movie! The Thing also took a long time to become a cult film. It wasn't appreciated much when it first came out.

(368) Charlie Heaton stayed in a grotty hostel for 'pilot' season in Los Angeles before Stranger Things.

(369) Winona Ryder says her favourite television show is The Americans - another series set in the 1980s.

(370) Billy's Camaro car in Stranger Things 2 has automatic windows in some scenes and crank windows in others.

(371) How did sound designer Craig Henighan go about creating the sound of the Upside Down? "I knew The Upside Down would be dark and swampy but I hadn't seen any visuals. In my first conversations with Matt and Ross, I tried to find out what this alternate reality would be like. Is it supposed to be reverberant? Is it supposed to be dead dry? You try to establish ground rules about what it is you're trying to create. They said it would be wet, and give the impression of being wet, but they're not going to be walking around in the swamp. It had to be spooky and haunting but at the same time be familiar. I worked with these great forest recordings with trees creaking and I tried to use a bit of comb filtering. I didn't want it to sound like it was comb filtered though. I didn't want it to have this robotic sort of sound. Using GRM Tools, I went through and adjusted filter settings and found one that gave me a sound that was not really a delay or a slap but just added a bit of enticement. It's something between a reverb and a delay. So I loop recorded long passages of me plunking around on my sampler with these different sound files. Then I re-sampled those, and then re-sampled them again.

By the second or third time, that's where the basis of The Upside Down sound happened. It developed from me imagining what this world would be, and when it came to applying it to the visuals, we don't get to see The Upside Down until late in the series. By the second or third time, that's where the basis of The Upside Down sound happened We open an episode with The Upside Down, and the camera turns, and that's when I thought, "Oh, this could really work." That's when all of the weird creaks and weird spores/soft ambiences came in. There's a bit of moaning in there. There's a bit of otherworldly winds. The big thing is everything is moving in those sequences and so I tried not to make anything sound static. That was a big payoff. To the Duffers credit, they didn't put music all over The Upside Down. They chose strategic spots for music. They let the sounds work, and that's half the trick, to have confidence in your sound design so that you don't need to put music everywhere. When the music does come in, it's there for a reason and it makes the scene more powerful. I can't say enough good things about Matt and Ross in terms of their confidence in our sound team. They let us come up with something that is unique but works so well with what they are doing and with their intentions."

(372) The Kellogg Company saw their stock price go up after the release of Stranger Things because of the demand for eggo waffles.

(373) Finn Wolfhard thinks Pennywise the clown from 'It' is scarier than the Demogorgon from Stranger Things.

(374) Winona Ryder liked the fact that Joyce wasn't your typical 'mom role'. "Usually the roles that you get offered that are the mom roles are very much the mom role. Literally, like standing in the doorway [Crosses arms], "Oh you kids!" with the fluffy slippers. This was different. She was much more than something to service the plot. So it was a really great opportunity."

(375) Many fans have commented that Natalie Portman looks like a grown up Millie Bobby Brown. Portman has embraced the apparent connection - playing Eleven in a Stranger Things sketch on Saturday Night Live. "I had met Millie at the Golden Globes a few months ago and she came up to me and was like, 'People keep telling me I look like the kid version of you!'" Portman told MTV News. "I see that there's something there, but I also find her, like, much more magical than I see myself. She's really wonderful."

(376) Gaten Matarazzo says his cleidocranial dysplasia has cost him parts as an actor. "My lisp, me being shorter, and having the teeth issue' meant writers couldn't 'write in my disability'."

(377) The Duffers described the different quests for the characters in terms of age in season one this way - "For the teens they're more in a classic horror film; John Carpenter's stuff like Halloween or Wes Craven's Nightmare on Elm Street. That's where the teens live. For the kids it's more the adventure thing, like The Goonies or Stand by Me. And then the adults are a bit more in the classic Spielberg movies like Close Encounters where they're slowly coming to realise that something extraordinary is happening around them and the sense of wonder that provokes. So that was what we were trying to do. Those are some of the big touchstones for us."

(378) Joe Keery says that he's starting to feel a little old to still be playing teenagers. "I still look relatively young for my age, so I find myself going in for these teenage roles. But as time goes on, I feel less and less like a teenager. Like I shouldn't be auditioning for a teenager. Certain things will always hurt: rejection, or loss. But I just turned 25. I'll be turning 26 this year. It's actually getting kind of far away for me. But I'm a working adult so if I've gotta be a teenager, I'll do it."

(379) Charlie Heaton says he prefers The Cure to The Clash - despite Jonathan's love of the latter.

(380) In the episode The Body, the scientist who enters the Upside Down is called Shephard. This is likely a reference to Alex Shepherd, the protagonist of Silent Hill.

(381) When Eleven enters the supermarket to steal the waffles in season one, you can see a couple of modern cars go past outside.

(382) In the early concept art for season one, the Demogorgon had a more humanoid looking face.

(383) Ross Duffer says Eleven was more violent in the original pilot script. "The Eleven character, the kind of powers she has and to have a young protagonist that's violent — it's not E.T. It's not a happy situation. She's killing people, and brutally murdering them. The original pilot was much more violent. It was originally like an R-rated thing."

(384) Steve's red bandana in the tunnels for Stranger Things 2 is a tribute to the red bandana worn by Josh Brolin in The Goonies.

(385) Stranger Things has a similar plot to a Richard Matheson penned Twilight Zone episode called Little Girl Lost. In the episode, a little girl gets trapped in another dimension.

(386) The smoke monster in Stranger Things 2 looks like it might have been inspired by Maman by the artist Louise Bourgeois.

Mamam is a bronze and marble sculpture that looks like a giant spider.

(387) David Harbour says it was tough to shoot the scene where Hopper and Eleven have a violent argument in the cabin in Stranger Things 2. "I had to work a lot harder while working with Millie, and I don't know exactly why. I think it's more complicated for me to yell at a young woman that way. It was very emotionally complex for me to play that. That was a really messed up day when we did that scene. I mean I was feeling all messed up about it. But I did want to treat the scene with the respect it deserves and I wanted to treat Millie with the respect she deserves as my female co-star, and really give her my all and my power, and she's able to give it right back. So that was a very complicated day."

(388) Mark Steger thinks there might be some plant DNA in the Demogorgon. "I feel like the monster maybe is more mushroom, which is kind of between plant and animal. Mushroom DNA is more similar to animal DNA than to plant DNA, [but the monster is] something else. He bleeds — or maybe they bleed, or she bleeds. I don't know what pronoun to use for the monster! But it feels like a little bit of both [plant and animal] to me."

(389) Steger says it was very difficult to hear directions in the Demogorgon suit. "It was actually really loud in there. Even when the motors were turned off, there was this high-pitched whine. And there were 26 motors running the head, and when we were actually doing a shot, I couldn't hear directions. They would have to shout at the top of their lungs, and then maybe I would hear them. The suit probably weighed about 30 pounds or so, and you're completely sealed in. It's like wearing a wetsuit and covering your whole body."

(390) Steger likens the Demogorgon to a shark. A natural hunter.

(391) The Duffers noticed David Harbour in a short lived series called Manhattan about the development of the first atomic bomb. "I've done a lot of stuff but I've never really been seen very broadly and so I had done this show called "Manhattan" where I was recurring and it was a show that Tommy Schlamme created and it was about guys building the atom bomb in Los Alamos in the early '40s and it was about these scientists and I played this guy Reed Akley, who was this scientist. He's kind of the villain. I was recurring on it and he's kind of the guy who has all this money and power and in the end you think he's gonna be able to solve their bomb problem and he sort of pretends like he does, and then at the end of the show you realize that he has no idea what's going on, he has kind of a breakdown. He really lied about a lot of it.

I don't know what specifically it was about that part but I remember asking them on set being like, "How did you guys know me?" And they were like, "'Manhattan.' 'Manhattan.'" So they had known some other work of mine, too, but they said that really secured them. And there was a kind of vulnerability to that character even though he had a strength to him. There was a kind of vulnerability and messed-up quality to him as he unravelled. Maybe that was it, but I don't know specifically, but I know that was the role that got them really interested."

(392) Shawn Levy says it was very different working on season two after all the fandom and interest generated by season one. "It's a very different experience. No one even cared what we were working on. We had this little show shooting in Atlanta with these twins that no one had ever heard of and a bunch of kids. So, we went from working in absolute anonymity to now working with, without question, a level of expectation and anticipation that is as daunting as it is exciting but for us the whole trick has been embracing the popularity of the show and appreciating it but knowing when it's time to put the blinders and the earplugs in and to quiet down that cultural noise and focus on the instincts that brought us here."

(393) The arc of Steve in season two as the all action babysitter wasn't written until four episodes had already been shot.

(394) The scene in Stranger Things 2 where Eleven shatters the windows in Hopper's cabin was done for real with practical effects and no stunt double for David Harbour. "[The Duffers] had scripted flinging the dictionary, shoving the couch, but all those door slams and things were things we had to come up with as we were shooting it," said Shawn Levy. "Our special effects crew had to figure it out on the fly. [And that part with the windows blowing out] That's real. No visual effects. We rigged all the windows. [David Harbour even did it himself].

We had blocked it in a way — we knew he would be facing that door, and so we knew his faces would be protected, and he did NOT want to use stunt double, and so that was all real."

(395) Winona Ryder says that when she was a kid she had a fantasy about living in a movie theatre! "The one that I had the fantasy about was this theater called The Plaza, and it was in this town that I lived in when I was 12 to 16. It was an old movie theater, and it was where I saw a lot of the big movies that had a big impact on me. It was just beautiful. I had this fantasy of taking out the seats and having a bed, and having a bicycle, so that I could get some exercise, and having a bathtub, and just never leaving. And maybe I'd put a kitchen somewhere in there. I was very young. It was a pipe dream. A lot of the old movie theaters are closing down now, which is really sad. It's still in the back of my mind."

(396) Noah Schnap played Tom Hanks son in the Steven Spielberg film Bridge of Spies. He admits that because he was so young he wasn't sure who Tom Hanks was.

(397) Gaten Matarazzo says he would like to go to college one day and that he likes history the most out of his school classes.

(398) For the crayon sketch drawings of Will in season two that form a map when strung together in the Byers house, the production designers had to map an Upside Down tunnel system that corresponded to a map of (the obviously fictional) Hawkins. This was tremendously complicated. "We invented a map of Hawkins last season and we refined it this season, so there is a working sense of what the geography of Hawkins is," said Chris Trujillo. "We had to hone in on how representational and true to scale what he was drawing could be, based on the square footage of the interior of the house and how big Hawkins is. We really did our best to try and ground it in some sort of consistent, rational physics."

(399) Winona Ryder and Paul Reiser have something in common in that they've both appeared in the Alien franchise.

(400) In Stranger Things 2, Erica Sinclair has a drawing of a rainbow and a sunflower on her wall. These are two of the words that Terry Ives recites on a constant loop because of her electro shock treatment at the Hawkins Lab.

(401) Ross Duffer says he wonders why the characters don't just leave crazy old Hawkins! "I don't know if we can justify something bad happening to them once a year. They're going to have to get the **** out of this town!"

(402) Matthew Modine suggested in an interview that Brenner might not necessarily be the despicable villain that we make him out to be. "Did he ever force Eleven to perform the experiments? Did he ever physically harm her? Was he always kind and careful to explain each test/experiment? Have you considered that the cat may have been a test to explore her empathy for another living creature? You perceive Dr Martin Brenner to be sinister. It's quite possible he is passionately pursuing Eleven simply because he knows her potential and worries what might or what could happen if she were to get in the hands of someone that is truly sinister."

(403) David Harbour says that, in real life, one of the things that scares him is the sea. "I'm terrified of the ocean. I think it's beautiful and magical, but I never go in. That deep, dark water, with no understanding of what goes on behind it — I think that's a metaphor for a lot of things. I'm terrified of the unknown, which is a driving force for me. I like this idea that the things that terrify us also draw us in."

(404) There was controversy when it was alleged that Sadie Sink was forced by the Duffers to kiss Caleb McLaughlin in the Snow Ball scene because they knew it would make her

uncomfortable. Sadie Sink later said the story was blown out of all proportion and that she'd been ok with the scene. "I always felt comfortable and the Duffer Brothers, they do the best job. And always create a comfortable space. And if I felt uncomfortable with anything, I wouldn't have done it."

(405) Sadie Sink added that it was also easier to do the scene because she already knew Caleb McLaughlin from living in New York and working on Broadway.

(406) Finn Wolfhard was hired for It before Stranger Things. If the film hadn't been delayed he might not have been able to do Stranger Things. "I had actually been hired to do It before Stranger Things — this was when Cary Fukunaga was going to direct and then pulled out. From there I got Stranger Things and then, when It came back with Andy Muschietti directing, I got the opportunity to audition again. It was a challenge in that Richie and Mike are completely different characters, but our version of It. And it's not a remake, by the way, it's the first feature adaptation of the Loser's part of the novel. Unlike Mr. King's novel, which is set in the 1950s, our version is set in the 1980s, like Stranger Things. So the cultural and political background is similar and maybe that makes it less challenging to play the two roles at a subconscious level. But Mike and Richie are just guys that I am pretending to be, with who I also have a lot in common personally, so that makes the whole process natural, too. If any of that makes sense."

(407) Sam Rockwell was considered as a candidate to play Chief Hopper.

(408) Although the Duffers say they didn't play Dungeons & Dragons as kids, they did play Magic: The Gathering. It was a similar game and played with cards.

(409) Billy's glorious mullet is mostly a wig worn at the sides and back by Dacre Montgomery.

(410) Dacre Montgomery says he was allowed a fair degree of input into the character of Billy. "I'd say it's 60/40 — 60 percent being on the Duffer side and 40 percent on mine. On the day, we'd change things because the narrative constantly changes. We're shooting episode five, and the Duffers haven't written seven, eight, and nine, so there are discussions that are had. That's what's so great about the two brothers: They are in an open forum with their actors, which provides everybody with an opportunity to evolve the character over a season rather than it being predetermined."

(411) Chris Trujillo says it was complex coming up with the look of the Upside Down "Dialling in a vision for the Upside Down (which we referred to as "the Nether" while conceptualizing it) was possibly the most creatively laborious and painstaking collaboration of the entire season. It was an object lesson in how tricky the alchemy of turning a shared fantasy into a physical set can be. It's funny because, from the beginning, everyone had a very clear sense of what the Upside Down should look and feel like and we could discuss it fairly clearly: like a dim, sick reflection of our world, murky darkness, a haze of "spores" floating in the gloom, vein-like vines overtaking all surfaces, like a disease is spreading over everything, etc, etc.

The Duffers even created a lengthy thoughtful document that does a damn good job of making strange sense of what the Upside Down is and how and why it came into existence, even a sort of physics that applies to it, but fabricating it was not so straightforward. From the outset, it was our intention to be as true as we could to the practical special effects that rose to the level of an art form during the era of film making we were so reverently trying to honour with Stranger Things. We all learned a lot about the advantages and limitations of that approach and gained a massive new appreciation for both practical effects artists and visual effects artists in the process.

Ultimately, we arrived at the Upside Down we all now know and love and fear through a lot of trial-and-error team work between physical effects and visual effects, with a large helping of creative construction, incredible scenic work, inspired lighting design and consummate camera work. The really magical part of creating the Upside Down, which actually works pretty well to sum up the entire film making process on Stranger Things, is that after all the logistical ups and downs, all the creative ins and outs, and after passing through a thousand different contributing hands, the world we found ourselves watching at the end of the process is exactly what we all hoped it would be."

(412) David Harbour says he would love to see a Hopper/Steve team up at some point in Stranger Things. "There's a certain aspect of Steve Harrington that I love so much; he's so damn eager to help out and there's even a little moment where we're at the thing and he says "the Germans" and Dustin's like, "the Nazis?" and he's like, "oh yeah, the Nazis, yeah." Like, I think Steve is kinda dumb? I love the fact that he's so great but kinda dumb, and I would love to play scenes with him where Hopper is just completely ripping him apart and then he walks away and Steve just calls him a dip**** under his breath or something. I would love to play more stuff with Joe, we'll have to see. There's just so many great characters on this show, it's hard to figure out a way to put Steve and Hopper together, but I'm sure the Duffers will figure it out, because I do love Joe, I love working with him."

(413) Dacre Montgomery says that Billy is a Stephen King inspired human antagonist. "Stephen King has this concept of humans being scarier than the supernatural, and the Duffer Brothers wanted to play around with that. So we meet initially and in the first half I am a stereotypical jock character, but in the second half I'm deeper. He was a great character to play around with and heavily oriented around Jack [Torrance] from The Shining with his unpredictable nature. I hope the

audience connects to that."

(414) David Harbour says that secrecy and privacy on the set of Stranger Things 2 was much more difficult compared to the production of season one. "We had to change the name of the show. We also had drones flying over, trying to get shots - I've never experienced that kind of madness before. There was a silly element to that."

(415) Winona Ryder had a four year relationship with Johnny Depp when she was a young actress.

(416) David Harbour says that shooting season two was a good decompression chamber for the kids because they were insulated from the sudden fame they have and were allowed to relax, goof around on the set and just be kids again.

(417) Stranger Things extras casting director Heather Taylor says she knew straight away that the show was going to be a success. "The moment I met the creators and the cast I knew it was going to be giant success. These kids have the most incredible personalities and are so unique- they also embody the traits of their characters, and are fantastic actors- that's a trifecta right there. There are no current shows out there that have a main cast of almost all kids, unless you're watching Disney or Nickelodeon (which is targeted for one specific age group). This show felt relatable to every age, from kids to adults. I would get totally lost from the outside world when I would read the scripts, not to mention how much everyone loves the 80s (including myself), how could this not be a hit!"

(418) The kids in the show say that Gaten Matarazzo is the biggest prankster on the set.

(419) Charlie Heaton says the original plan in season one was for Jonathan to end up with Nancy and this was even a part of his screen test. "In the screen test there was a scene where

Nancy and Jonathan - that relationship happens originally. They got together, there was a kissing scene in the screen test. But the way they've done it was much more interesting, and a credit to Joe's acting."

(420) The Duffer Brothers were held back a year in school because they refused to mix with other children.

(421) Sean Astin says he approached the creators of Stranger Things for a part in the show.

(422) In the fight scene between Billy and Steve in the finale of season two, Joe Keery was hurt for real when the plate was smashed over his head. This take was used in the final edit.

(423) Stranger Things has a rather international cast despite its very American setting. Millie Bobby Brown and Charlie Heaton are British, Dacre Montgomery is Australian, Finn Wolfhard is Canadian, and Linnea Berthelse is Danish.

(424) The cast called Finn 'Emo Mike' in season two because Mike is quite sulky and depressed at the loss of Eleven.

(425) Musician Father John Misty a.k.a Josh Tillman says he turned down an invitation to audition for Stranger Things 2 because he didn't want to be "TV famous".

(426) Millie Bobby Brown came up with Eleven's 'head snap' for when she kills the orderlies in the lab and breaks Troy's arm.

(427) Stranger Things was launched on Netflix on July 15, 2016.

(428) Caleb McClaughlin asked to wear a camouflage bandana in season one.

(429) In the episode 'Trick or Treat, Freak', Jonathan mistakes a girl dressed as Siouxsie Sioux for a Kiss fan at the party.

Siouxsie Sioux was the lead singer of punk group Siouxsie and the Banshees.

(430) The bus scene in The Bathtub was a chore to shoot because the boys broke wind! "We're shooting a scene in the abandoned bus, and one of the boys decides to fart," said the Duffers. "More than once. It became so toxic in the bus that the crew had to temporarily evacuate. We had a pep talk the next day that basically boiled down to: 'We're right at the end. Don't drop the ball. Let's bring this home.'"

(431) Millie Bobby Brown nearly quit acting before she got the part of Eleven in Stranger Things.

(432) Dustin's 'do you like these pearls?' growl/purr in season two is based on Gaten Matarazzo's impression of Chewbacca from Star Wars.

(433) Priah Ferguson, who plays Erica Sinclair, was given more lines and screen time than originally intended because the Duffers thought the child actress was so funny.

(434) The fleshly fanged face petals on the Demogorgon in season one were designed so that they never repeated a set pattern. They had to appear natural and unpredictable.

(435) Chris Trujillo says they had a relatively modest budget of $220,000 to secure the time specific eighties props for season one.

(436) Propmaster Lynda Reiss says a lot of research went into Dungeons & Dragons before the first season. "In order to be authentic to the game and honour the fans we really did a lot of research on D&D. We visited a group that still meets to play

the game, and even found original campaign books with drawings from a guy who was a kid in the Eighties. You can see them on Mike Wheeler's bedroom wall."

(437) The props department had to get multiple copies of Jonathan's Pentax MX camera for the camera smash scene in season one.

(438) The props department wanted Mike to wear an E.T. watch but it was too expensive to get the rights.

(439) You may notice that Dustin's bike is made up of two different colours. "With Dustin's bike, we decided he was sort of a klutz. So we painted his bike but never finished it, and that's why his bike is two colours," says Lynda Reiss.

(440) Winona Ryder's favourite book is The Catcher in the Rye by JD Salinger.

(441) Many of the cast of Stranger Things have appeared in music videos. Winona Ryder and Matthew Modine (as we have mentioned) for Roy Orbison but also Millie Bobby Brown in Sigma's Find Me and later the xx's I Dare You, Gaten Matarazzo in Katy Perry's Swish Swish, Finn Wolfhard in Spendtime Palace's Sonora, and Natalia Dyer for James Bay's Wild love.

(442) Mrs Wheeler is reading Johanna Lindsey's Heart of Thunder in the bath when Billy knocks on the door in the finale of Stranger Things 2. Lindsey is the author of many popular historical romance novels.

(443) In the last shot of Stranger Things 2, when the screen tilts Upside Down, the cars seem to change from modern to more vintage 50s style models.

(444) Jonathan seems to wear a Timex Weekender watch in

season one.

(445) The makeup department needed seventy wigs for the extras in the Halloween party scene in Stranger Things 2. The extras either had to have a costume or eighties hair so a lot of wigs were needed.

(446) Amy Seimetz, who plays Becky Ives, says she impersonated her grandmother to get into the character! "As soon as they put me in the costume and did my hair, I sent this photo to my entire family, and I'm like "Oh my god, I look like my aunt and my grandma," specifically during this era. Sometimes when you perform, you don't know what path you're going to take, or what character you want to portray. As soon as I got in the costume, I knew I was so doing an impersonation of my grandma … she was a very complicated lady, and not the warmest. Sort of a brassy lady. So, as soon as I got in costume, I knew I had to do a Grandma Seimetz impersonation. I definitely called upon childhood to bring forth Becky."

(447) Sean Astin provided an entertaining description of how the heroic demise of Bob was shot. "The Duffers luxuriate in their storytelling, building suspense and creating those jump-out-of-your-skin moments. For the running stuff, I'd either chase a golf cart down the hall or the golf cart would chase me, with a camera rig on the side. To watch it [on set] you'd just think, "Oh, it's just a guy and a golf cart." But when you'd look through the monitor, it would look so cool! The magic is in the cinematography; Tim Ives [the director of photography] is as much a character in the show as Eleven. The biting scene was exhausting for everybody. It took a long time to shoot, and there was a lot of screaming and writhing on the ground. They put dots all over you, and at one point one of the writers got on top of me and I writhed with them so that my clothes would crinkle up. They painted them out so all you can see is me. Then they brought in this crane thing for the blood

spurting out of the mouth. It was a big sequence to do, and a heck of a send-off. I remember hoping that if I got killed off the show, it would be memorable. I think there's a chance that people will look back at Season 2 and go, "Oh right — Bob's the guy who got eaten by the dogs!""

(448) The hairstylist on Stranger Things says that Millie Bobby Brown kept discarding the blonde wig that Eleven wears briefly in season one. "One time, last year, she was so sick of the blonde wig, I found it hanging on a tree branch, hanging in the wind. I was like, 'Oh my god, girl! You can't do that to me!'"

(449) The Byers home and Hawkins Lab interiors were shot at EUE/Screen Gems Studios Atlanta, 175 Lakewood Way, Atlanta.

(450) EUE/Screen Gems Studios is a 10-stage, 33-acre Atlanta studio complex with sound stages which offers 250,000 sq ft of production space and 50,000 sq ft of furnished office space. Opened in 2010 by the Cooney family, the studios are ten minutes away from Hartsfield-Jackson Atlanta International Airport.

(451) The real life location for Lonnie Byers' house was 930 Garibaldi Street Southwest, Atlanta.

(452) The scenes in season one where the boys walk the train tracks was shot at Stone Mountain Park.

(453) The mouth of the Demogorgon is based on a snapping turtle.

(454) 3D printers were used to create a model of what the Demogorgon would look like.

(455) Shawn Levy says that Stranger Things is headed by a

remarkably small team for a show this big and popular. "There's no studio, there's no outside showrunner, there's no big TV company. There's literally [producer] Dan Cohen, me, the Duffer Brothers and we deal with three execs at Netflix. This TV show is made by a smaller team than almost any TV show or movie I've ever heard of."

(456) Aimee Mullins, who plays Terry Ives, was born with fibular hemimelia (missing fibula bones) and as a result had both of her legs amputated below the knee when she was one. She competed as an athlete in the 1996 Para-Olympic Games. "I've had journalists asking me what do we call you - is it handicapped , are you disabled, physically challenged? I said well hopefully you could just call me Aimee. But if you have to describe it, I'm a bilateral below the knee amputee."

(457) Stranger Things 2 is set just before the 1984 presidential election. The Wheelers have a Reagan sign while Dustin's mother is supporting Walter Mondale.

(458) Gaten Matarazzo said the three candy bars he likes best are Three Musketeers, Charleston Chew and Reese's Fast Break.

(459) The package of cameras used to make Stranger Things is as follows - RED Epic Dragon (Season 1), RED Weapon Helium (Season 2), Leica Summilux-C lenses, Redcode RAW (6K and 8K).

(460) From 1947 to 2012 the Heathkit company produced a range of kits from basic oscilloscopes to ham radios.

(461) Ross Duffer says he knew that Stranger Things would not work if they didn't find the right child actors. "We knew right away that if we didn't get the right kid actors, the show would fall apart. There's really nothing worse than a bad child performance, so we needed them to be great. Once the show

got the green light, we just started looking for kids. We only had one script written, but we used sides from Stand By Me and made up some other sides, just to get it going. These kids flooded in with takes and our casting director Carmen Cuba would weed through some of them. I think it was about 900 kids or something. But actually, it's not an impossible task where you're like, "Oh, what do we do? Is it this kid? Is it that kid?" You can tell within five or 10 seconds of a kid performing. So you just skip to the next, skip to the next, skip to the next. Because you're just looking for something authentic, and most kids don't have it. They're the ones that are obviously well-trained, but it feels like Disney, where they're winking at the camera."

(462) The Duffers say they are not sure if they are identical twins.

(463) Noah Schnapp had this response to speculation on Instagram that his character Will is gay. "I think everyone here is missing the point. An author called Gary Schmidt came to speak at our school this week and he said that good stories aren't supposed to leave you with answers because then you never question yourself and you forget about it. A good book, or a good show leaves a lot of unanswered questions but makes you think. Which is what you are all doing. For me, Will being gay or not is besides the point. Stranger Things is a show about a bunch of kids who are outsiders and find each other because they have been bullied in some way or are different. Does being sensitive, or a loner, or a teenager who likes photography, or a girl with red hair and big glasses, make you gay? I'm only 12 but I do know we all relate to being different. And that's why I think the Duffers wrote the show the way they did. So you can ask all these questions. I hope the real answer never comes out!"

(464) The Duffers say they know how they want Stranger Things to end. "Once we got into the room for season two, we

started expanding our mythology. We never got boxed in, because we're dealing with an alternate dimension. It feels like the possibilities are limitless. We're building up the mythology in a way that we know now where we want the story and these characters to end."

(465) Kim Wilcox, the costume designer for season two, spilled the beans on Eleven's punk makeover. "What I wanted to do was find something that would be slightly more pop culture but still punk. If you remember in the '80s, Madonna was famous for wearing these blazers, rolling up the sleeves and popping the collar. Madonna stole that from the punks, so it's kind of a hand-me-down already. We definitely tried a few different kind of jackets on and this was the one that definitely spoke the most to us. It made a lot of sense for her. The thing about that jacket is it feels a lot older than it is. We needed something that we felt like, in the '80s, when you were looking in the thrift store and your parents' closet, the things you thought were cool was from the '60s. So if you were thrifting, that's what you would pick. So we wanted something that actually felt much older than the '80s, but that would make sense for her."

(466) Sadie Sink says that sudden fame can be quite overwhelming at times. "A lot of people have been telling me — as far as social media goes — my followers will go up! I'm not really looking forward to that, just because like it's kind of scary in a way. The other kids were saying, 'Oh my God, just wait! It's going to get crazy — like with what happened with us!' Caleb told me you go to bed and essentially wake up in the morning with 100,000 more followers! So I turned off my notifications."

(467) Kim Wilcox says that the look of Nancy evolved in season two. "She's evolving, she's becoming a woman. In the first couple of episodes, she's trying to be normal, but it's not normal for her - there's just a lot that she goes through this

season that we wanted to make sure that she grew. We wanted to take her out of the prim and proper plaid cardigan and skirt set, and start working her into jeans. It's really fun to see her grow and for that journey to be reflected in the costumes as well."

(468) In Stranger Things 2, Eleven is watching 1931's Frankenstein in the cabin while she waits for Hopper.

(469) Dustin's puffed up hair at the Snow Ball is based on Jon Cryer in the John Hughes film Pretty in Pink.

(470) Kyle Lambert did the sketching for his iconic Stranger Things posters using Procreate on an iPad Pro with an Apple Pencil.

(471) Practically every character in season one wears corduroy at some point!

(472) Barb wears high wasted Levi jeans in season one.

(473) Nancy goes from blouses and cardigans to a shearling jacket when she becomes an action heroine in season one.

(474) The Clash song Should I Stay or Should I Go appeared on their 1982 album Combat Rock.

(475) The Wheeler house has a wood-panelled station wagon outside in season one.

(476) Matt Duffer says that he thinks Dr Brenner is still alive. "I would say that if we were going to kill Brenner - as an audience member watching the show, if that was his death, that would be very unsatisfying to me — when the monster jumps on him and we cut away. He would deserve much more than that as an ending. So yes, there's a possibility of seeing him again."

(477) Winona Ryder, according to Shawn Levy, cried for a grand total of ten hours all in all during the production of the Christmas lights scenes in season one.

(478) Shawn Levy says that not every reference or touchstone in Stranger Things is planned. Some happen by accident. "The Duffers and I are always amused at how everyone assumes that the visual referencing is super conscious and deliberate. That Spielbergian, Stephen King '80s cinema runs through our veins. Those images are baked into our film nerd DNA."

(479) Winona Ryder did the scene where Joyce paints an Ouija alphabet on the wall in one take.

(480) Eleven was supposed to have a completely shaven head in the early plan for Stranger Things but they felt this would make the character look too aggressive and so went for a buzzcut instead.

(481) The original idea for the Christmas lights in season one was that Jonathan and Nancy were going to use them to track the monster.

(482) As a gift, Winona Ryder gave Charlie Heaton a Clash t-shirt that she had worn when she was his age.

(483) Season two costume designer Kim Wilcox says she scoured Tiger Beat and Cosmopolitan magazines, as well as old Sears and J.C. Penney's catalogues for inspiration.

(484) Kim Wilcox said the fashion of the individual boys at the Snow Ball dance is a hint to their futures. Dustin is wearing a bow tie. Might that mean an academic future lies ahead for Dustin?

(485) The toddlers on the set of season one were told the

Demogorgon was from Monsters Inc so they wouldn't be afraid of it.

(486) Ross Duffer says that the fact they had a limited budget on season one made the show better because they had to be more creative. A case in point was the void sequences featuring Eleven. "What we were trying to do was come up with a visual representation for being in Eleven's head. And [the emptiness of the Void] is just a way to sort of get that across in a very simple way that obviously is not going to be involving heavy [visual effects] like in the 'X-Men' movies with Professor X. And again, you know, I think it's one of those things where the limitations of [having] a TV schedule and budget made us be more creative."

(487) Ross Duffer says it was surprisingly cheap and easy to shoot the void sequences with Eleven "It's just an inch of water on the ground, and then we just hung up black curtains, and suddenly we're in Eleven's head. It's cool how you can achieve something that we think is such a big idea so simply."

(488) Charlie Heaton had to wear front hair extensions in season one because he singed his hair on a candle in the bath.

(489) Kim Wilcox says she dressed a lot of the school extras in pastel shades to reflect films from this era.

(490) A company called Yandy caused controversy when they released an 'Upside Down Honey Costume' that resembled the iconic clothes worn by Eleven in season one. The costume was described by Yandy this way - "Evade your enemies in this Upside Down Honey costume featuring a powder pink babydoll dress, white buttons accents, a navy bomber jacket with long sleeves, white thigh high socks with striped tops, and a waffle purse."

(491) When Will is found in the quarry river in season one, his

'body' is not a dummy but a stuntwoman dressed in Will's clothing.

(492) Kimberly Adams, costume designer on season one, explained how she approached the clothes to be worn by Steve and Nancy.

"Everyone has experienced the high school classes and it was important to capture those variations in characters. Nancy was such fun to fit! Natalia [Dyer] enjoyed trying on period clothing and discovering her character. I took some inspiration from my high school years but in the context of a Midwest girl as opposed to West Coast girl that I was. Her family is upper middle class, she is smart and sweet and feminine and her closet needed to reflect that. Steve comes from a wealthy family and was what we called a 'prep' in high school, preppy and cool. Polo shirts, Levi's, khakis, and Brooks Brothers basics worn with attitude!"

(493) In the finale of season two, Steve finds the infamous Christmas lights from season one while he is rummaging around.

(494) Millie Bobby Brown's old primary school teacher in England says she knew Millie would be famous one day.

(495) When Eleven uses the television to enter the void in season two this is an obvious reference to Poltergeist.

(496) The Duffers say they play a lot of survival horror games in their spare time.

(497) A possible plot hole in season one is how on earth did the Hawkins Lab make the dummy of Will so accurately and so quickly?

(498) In 2017, a Stranger Things computer game was made by

by Texas studio BonusXP, Inc. and published by Netflix. The game was deliberately retro.

(499) In the computer game, Max Mayfield has Psychic powers.

(500) Linnea Berthelse had only acted in short films when she was cast as Kali but Shawn Levy said that when they cast for Stranger Things they just look for actors they find interesting regardless of how much experience they may or may not have.

(501) In season one, Hopper has a Motorola walkie-talkie which seems far too modern for 1983.

(502) In season one, Will seems excited at the thought of getting an Atari console. But Atari was already old by 1983 and it probably would have been more realistic if the boys were more excited by the thought of a Commodore 64.

(503) The Duffers say that Eleven was the most difficult role to cast in Stranger Things. "Eleven was the most difficult role to cast because she has to convey many emotions with very little dialogue. Child actors, even the great ones, almost always have difficulty listening. They're able to deliver their lines well, but to stay fully in character in a scene when they're not talking - that's another skill set entirely. They're kids after all; focus is not their strong suit. To find a girl who didn't just have this skill but excelled at it made us concerned. Then we met Millie Bobby Brown, and we weren't so concerned anymore."

(504) The dummy of Will in season one was built by Justin Raleigh. The Duffers - "It was a fake corpse built by a talented artist named Justin Raleigh, whose company Fractured FX builds prosthetics for many hit shows, including one of our personal favourites, Steven Soderbergh's The Knick."

(505) Raleigh's dummies are so realistic that that the Boston Children's Hospital now has him build simulation bodies to train their surgeons!

(506) The Duffers used the dummy of Will to play a rather dark prank on Noah Schnapp's mother. "We immediately took Noah's mom aside, told her we had something to show her, and led her into a dark closet where we had propped up this frighteningly realistic corpse of her son. She was startled at first, and we felt like maybe we crossed a line... But after the initial shock, she loved it. Before long, she was taking pictures with her child's fake corpse and texting the photos to all her friends. Yeah, Noah has a pretty cool mom."

(507) The visual effects for the first season finale were only turned in a few weeks before Stranger Things was launched on Netflix.

(508) The Duffers say that in preparation for Stranger Things 2 they watched their favourite movie sequels for inspiration. The Empire Strikes Back, Godfather Part II, Aliens, Toy Story 2, Evil Dead 2, and Indiana Jones and the Temple of Doom.

(509) The first scene written and shot for the show was the boys playing Dungeons & Dragons in Mike's basement den.

(510) In the season two episode The Pollywog, Dustin consults a field guide to reptiles and amphibians and suggests Indirana semipalmata as the species of frog that Dart could be. However, Indirana semipalmata wasn't classified as a term until 1986.

(511) In The Vanishing of Will Byers we see a type of Bluebird school bus that was not in service until the 1990s.

(512) The Duffers say they wanted the Demogorgon to have a

slender body just like the Xenomorph in the Alien films.

(513) The elements in Mr Clarke's periodic table that weren't discovered yet in 1984 include Darmstadtium (Ds), Roentgenium (Rg), Copernicium (Cn), Ununtrium (Uut), Flerovium (Fl), Ununpentium (Uup), Livermorium (Lv), Ununseptium (Uus) and Ununoctium (Uuo).

(514) Although - in contrast - the scientific t-shirt that Dustin wears in the arcade scene does have 1970s elements.

(515) In the CPR for Will in the first season finale, Hopper does 30:2. From 1974 to 2005 it was 15:2 chest compression:ventilation.

(516) When Emma Watson was introduced to the kids from the It movie starring Finn Wolfhard she presumed they were the Stranger Things kids. She obviously hadn't watched the show!

(517) When they watched the early episodes of season two, a lot of fans were convinced that Bob Newby was going to turn out to be a villain.

(518) David Harbour says that one of the big inspirations for Hopper is Nick Nolte in old cop movies.

(519) The Stranger Things theme sounds similar to the second tune on the Tron: Legacy soundtrack by Daft Punk.

(520) Netflix didn't want the kids to swear in season two but the Duffers managed to keep the swear words in.

(521) The Duffers say the kids swear much more in real life than they do in Stranger Things!

(522) Joe Keery estimates that he had 100 failed auditions as an

actor before he started getting some work.

(523) The character that became Kali was originally going to be a 30 year-old man.

(524) Millie Bobby Brown says her dream role is to play young Princess Leia in a Star Wars film.

(525) Chris Trujillo landed Stranger Things after working on Honeymoon, an indie horror film directed by Leigh Janiak — the wife of Ross Duffer.

(526) These Chevrolet Caprice police cars seen at the start of Stranger Things 2 have wide rectangular headlights which did not come into service until 1987.

(527) In season one and two, Hopper wears the hairband of his daughter Sara on his wrist. We saw Sara had this blue hairband in her hair in flashback scenes. In the finale of season two, Eleven is wearing the hairband on her wrist when she dances with Mike.

(528) The Duffers say that the outrage at the apparent lack of concern for the missing Barb in season one slightly misses the fact that the events of season one are supposed to take place over several days - a relatively short span of time.

(529) Stranger Things seems inspired in part by the 1980 Ken Russell film Altered States - which also features sensory deprivation experiments.

(530) Shawn Levy picked the Peter Gabriel cover of David Bowie's Heroes to play in the episode Holly Jolly.

(531) David Harbour felt that the end of The Body, when Hopper snips the fence of the Hawkins Lab to signal he is about to sneak in, would be anti-climactic. The Duffers

assured him that with the right sound effects it would "badass".

(532) The Duffers say that one of their favourite sequences in season one is the start of The Flea and the Acrobat when we cross-cut between Hopper in the lab and the boys pondering the Upside Down.

(533) The Duffers cut a fake trailer not only to pitch Stranger Things but also test if a synth score would work in Spielberg style scenes. "To test-drive the concept, we threw together a quick mock-trailer for the show, editing together clips from more than 25 classic films. We then scored this fake trailer with John Carpenter music, using some of our favourite songs from The Fog to Escape From New York. As soon as we heard John Carpenter's eerie synth drones play over shots from E.T., we got major goosebumps. It worked, big time."

(534) Michael Stein of Survive had a day job selling used synthesizers when he was asked to do the Stranger Things music.

(535) The Duffers say they quickly became in awe of Millie Bobby Brown after they cast her. "Millie's something special, alright, with a downright spooky preternatural talent. She inhabits every moment so intensely, with some alchemy of intelligence, preparation, and instinct. By the end of production, we found ourselves listening to Millie as if she were one of our most seasoned adult actors."

(536) The Duffers say that Hellraiser and the fiction and films of Clive Barker in general were an influence on Stranger Things.

(537) The Demogorgon was built by Spectral Motion. The company had previously worked on Guillermo del Toro's Hellboy films.

(538) In the finale of season one, Mike rather than Dustin was supposed to carry the exhausted Eleven into the classroom but Finn Wolfhard wasn't strong enough to run carrying Millie Bobby Brown so Gaten Matarazzo did it instead.

(539) In the bike chase in season one, the boys mention "Elm and Cherry" as a meeting point. This seems a likely reference to A Nightmare On Elm Street.

(540) In Stranger Things 2, Dustin has a certificate of Anti-Paranormal Proficiency on his wall from the Ghostbusters official fan club.

(541) In Stranger Things 2, one of the men from the lab says "stay frosty" as the soldiers prepare to enter the tunnels. This is a famous quote taken directly from James Cameron's Aliens.

(542) The second season required many more visual effects than the first season.

(543) The Duffers say they enjoy shooting around the Atlanta area because it reminds them of their childhood home of North Carolina.

(544) Justin Doble, one of the writers on Stranger Things, got his start in the industry writing for the JJ Abrams show Fringe.

(545) Matt Duffer defended The Lost Sister after the episode received a fair degree of criticism. "It's important for Ross and I to try stuff and not feel like we're doing the same thing over and over again. It's almost like doing a whole little other pilot episode in the middle of your season, which is kind of a crazy thing to do. But it was really fun to write and cast and work on."

(546) The article we see on a wall in The Lost Sister about Ray

Carroll is patently fake as it simply repeats the same passage over and over again. A familiar movie trick for fake articles that the viewer can barely see. The passage it repeats is - "Long standing employee Ray Carroll spent his last few hours at Hawkins National Labs strolling the hallways and saying his goodbyes. Ray started as an orderly in the hospital wing of Hawkins back in 1969. He was honourably discharged from the Army Medical Corp after three years in Vietnam working in the MASH units. Ray took the night school degree courses offered by the DOE so he could advance thru the Hawkins System. He finished up as a fully qualified ECT Therapist, working in the Pediatric Unit of the Hawkins Research Hospital. Ray worked closely with several of Hawkins research doctors in the Parapsychology Department."

(547) The shots of Steve and kids in the tunnels in Stranger Things 2 are deliberately designed to evoke the iconography of the Richard Donner/Steven Spielberg film The Goonies.

(548) Millie Bobby Brown said in an interview on Colbert that one of her own personal fears is bungalows. She said she finds the concept of a house with no stairs strangely disturbing!

(549) Joe Keery says he only washes his famous hair once every three days.

(550) David Harbour says he loved the fact that some viewers didn't like Hopper at first because it gave the character a redemptive hero arc to go on.

(551) Gaten Matarazzo's voice changed during the production of season one so he couldn't be used to dub any of his own dialogue in post-production.

(552) The scene in The Flea and the Acrobat where the deer is suddenly yanked away from Steve and Nancy by an unseen presence is a carbon copy of a scene in the interactive horror

video game Until Dawn.

(553) One crazy fan theory about Stranger Things 2 is that Max and Billy are part of a family of Soviet spies secretly embedded in the United States!

(554) The arcade scenes in Stranger Things 2 were deemed too 'pretty' by some gamers who remember real eighties video arcades. They remembered arcades having bare walls and generally being dirtier and slightly more drab places than depicted in Stranger Things.

(555) The story arc of the first season is foreshadowed by the game of Dungeons & Dragons the boys play early on.

(556) David Harbour said he did some method acting at the start of season one. When production started, he was deliberately aloof and kept his distance from the children for a time to get into the character of the grouchy Hopper.

(557) In the original script for the pilot, Joyce was much louder and more brassy. This was toned down when Winona Ryder was cast in the part.

(558) In Stranger Things 2, we see a flashback where Hopper takes Eleven to his grandfather's cabin to hide her and then starts dancing when he plays some music to tidy the cabin up to. Hopper is dancing to (the appropriately titled) 'You Don't Mess Around With Jim' by Jim Croce. Harbour was quite amused that Hopper dancing became a popular meme. "I just had no idea or expectations that the 'dad dancing' or 'white man Hopper dancing' was going to take off. It was funny, when we shot that scene it was supposed to be a bit more serious than it was. I remember talking to [Shawn Levy, the episode's director] and they had this other song for it. But I love Jim Croce and I thought Hopper would to."

(559) David Harbour loves the reaction of Eleven to his 'dad dancing' scene. "I mean she's a little alien telekinetic girl, so I don't know that she's ever seen a grown man in full khakis dancing before," Harbour said. "I imagine that would be very assaulting and confusing. Even if you've been locked in a room playing mind games your whole life, that might be the scariest thing you've ever seen."

(560) Naomi Watts and Marisa Tomei were names considered for the part of Joyce in the very early stages of Stranger Things.

(561) In Stranger Things 2, when Will tells Joyce he felt the Mind Flayer "everywhere", Shawn Levy told Noah Schnapp to whisper the word "everywhere" to make it more ominous.

(562) The end of Stranger Things 2 originally had some 'easter eggs' to set up season three but these were abandoned as the Duffers didn't want themselves to feel 'boxed-in'.

(563) The Police song 'Every Breath You Take' which plays at the end of Stranger Things 2 is about stalking. It was written as a sinister love song. The song was chosen to indicate the Mind Flayer is still stalking the people of Hawkins.

(564) Millie Bobby Brown described her casting as Eleven this way - "I was living in London at that time. I was at my house, just watching TV, and my parents were like, "There's this show called Montauk. It's supposed to be really great. They haven't even written the first episode yet, but they want you to audition for it. It's going to be a good show." I was doing the tape for it, and I just loved it. They called me back, and I was doing another tape for them. They called me back again. They took that tape and then they were like, "Alright, we want to do a Skype meeting with you now." We didn't talk about the show once. We actually spoke about '80s movies and were talking about what my favourite things to do are,

and what music I listen to. Then they were like, "Alright, we want you to fly to LA," and I was like, "Wow, okay. They must be serious about this now." I went into the office and I saw one boy, one girl, Finn [Wolfhard], and then there was me. I went in with this other boy, and then the other boy left and Finn came in, and I was like, "Wow, Finn is way better than the other boy. Finn has to get this job." Then, we all got to experiment, and they just thought Finn and I were the perfect match to work with each other. The next day, on a Monday, they called me up and said, "Can you be our Eleven?" and I was like, "Yes, I can.""

(565) Randy Havens doubts that he would have the qualities to be a teacher in real life. "I am definitely not as kind as he is. It's something I aspire to in my life, but it's hard sometimes to be that open and loving. I love kids. My niece is almost four and she is legit my favorite person in the world. I don't have the patience to work within the school system right now. I think it's really challenging to be a teacher and it takes a really special person to be able to do that. So for all the teachers out there, you have my respect and admiration."

(566) Millie Bobby Brown says that - strangely - it is sometimes more challenging to play a part that doesn't have much dialogue. "I find it more difficult than actually having [a lot of] dialogue. Because if I have dialogue, I'm more focused on the dialogue. But with my actions, you know, I have to cry sometimes, and even if I don't have to cry, I well up because she's so emotional."

(567) Chesting Rushing, who plays Steve's odious friend Tommy, is nothing like the nasty character he plays in Stranger Things. In real life, Rushing speaks out against bullying in schools and helped to start a sensory theatre for special needs children.

(568) Randy Havens says that Millie Bobby Brown was sick

the day he shot some of the scene where Mr Clarke surprises Eleven and the boys outside the AV room so he had to do part of the scene with a stand in for her.

(569) Gaten Matarazzo says he has a lot of the curiosity of Dustin and tends to ask his teachers a lot of questions.

(570) The Duffers say it was always their dream to design and create a famous monster and so working on the Demogorgon fulfilled that.

(571) Did you notice the egg that the Demogorgon is crouching over in season one? Aaron Sims, the concept artist, said this - "Little was made of the hollowed-out "egg" that Hopper seemed to find in the finale's Upside Down search for Will, leading many to speculate the creature might somehow have reproduced in time for Season 2. As it turns out – we've actually seen that "egg" before without realizing: The egg was a design for something you actually see a couple times in the show, whether you recognize it or not. There are a couple encounters where we see the Demogorgon hunkered over, eating something - when Nancy goes into the Upside-Down through the tree, and when Eleven finds the creature in her "vision", it's hunkered over this egg, feeding off of it. It's not clear whether or not this is the creature's offspring - we don't even know if it's the same species. The only info we have is that the creature is feeding off this egg somehow."

(572) Millie Bobby Brown says she would love to be in a comedy one day rather than always play the troubled supernatural girl.

(573) Guillermo del Toro loved Stranger Things and said - "Stranger Things may be a lot of things: King, Spielberg, 80's, myself, but what it is, above all, is good!!"

(574) When Will tells Joyce he doesn't get scared anymore

when she surprises him with Poltergeist tickets, she says "Oh yeah? Not even of... clowns?" This is an obvious reference to Stephen King's IT.

(575) Randy Havens says that he didn't study science to play Mr Clarke. "The important thing for me as an actor was to find the emotional truth of a character like Mr Clarke, since I knew there was no way that I was gonna become as smart as he is. So I focused on the thing that I could understand: that Mr Clarke identified with Mike, Dustin, Lucas and Will because he was like them when he was young. Maybe he felt like an outcast or was bullied and he wanted to create a safe place where his students felt they belonged."

(576) David Harbour says of the dummy of Will that Hopper cuts into in season one that "it was hard to cut and felt super gross."

(577) Priah Ferguson said she was cast as Erica this way - "My agents at People Store send over audition requests called a breakdown. Most times a breakdown will give you a lot of information about the character, but it only described Erica as "Lucas' little sister. She thinks he and his friends are nerds." That gave me some room to explore the character, plus I like to improv. When I read the script, I loved the character, the writing, and I had heard great things about the show. I really just wanted to show my best work. The audition tape was due within two days but I submitted it in 24hrs, I wanted to get it in early lol. Two weeks later, my agent called to let me know I booked it! My mom and I started screaming and jumping around. Although it was a minor role, just to be chosen to work on Stranger Things felt like a dream. It still feels like a dream."

(578) Millie Bobby Brown says that when she auditioned and was cast in Stranger Things she had no idea that Eleven was going to have super powers.

(579) David Harbour says that if he could choose any five dinner guests from history they would be - Shakespeare, Dante, Meville, Nabakov and Steve Martin.

(580) Linnea Berthelsen says there was no specific character called Kali when she auditioned. "There wasn't really a character that I was auditioning [for]. It was more like they wanted to create a character based on a few things and had a vague idea about where they wanted it to go, but they didn't really have a clear image of what they wanted to do — at least that's how I felt about it. [I auditioned with] three different scenes and tried to figure it out, like 'How can I create something based on the first season and the dynamic?' I had to create the background story, kind of fill in the gaps. I had no idea it was going to be Eleven's sister, and I had no idea she was going to have superpowers. No one confirmed it until the screen test."

(581) Glennellen Anderson, who plays Nicole in episodes 3 and 6 of season one, auditioned for the part of Barb.

(582) Catherine Dyer says that she loved playing Agent Connie Frazier in season one. "I've seen the whole series & loved every minute of it...even if I hadn't been in it! I loved the shock of Connie shooting Benny - I feel that scene really set the tone for the show. No one knew what to expect. And yes, every time Connie came to the door you didn't know what to expect! I loved the first scene where Connie shoots Benny. As an actor it was a tad unsettling aiming a gun at a person especially someone as nice as Chris Sullivan (Benny)."

(583) Aaron Sims says the Upside Down portals were 'too sci-fi' in the early concept art and so were changed to be more biological. "The only thing that really evolved was the opening in the lab - the rift to the Upside-Down. That portal was an explorational process that went through variations of

looks and feels. Many of the early designs felt too sci-fi; we wanted it to feel grounded, somewhat disgusting, like looking at the inside of a body. As opposed to a portal to a parallel universe, this felt like a membrane, like a physical organ."

(584) Hazy Shade of Winter by The Bangles, which we hear in the 1983 set episode two, was recorded in 1987.

(585) Priah Ferguson says she was allowed to improvise a little when playing Erica. "Working with the Duffer brothers was a blast. While filming, sometimes they would come up with a new idea for Erica. They would share it with me and just let me go with it. When I'm working, or in the zone, I'll improv or ad lib just here and there. It's not always on purpose or planned, but if it feels right I'll go for it. I appreciate them for giving me space to do that, especially as a child actor. It really makes me feel connected and I'm grateful they trust my work. Oh, they took me and my mom on a set tour. It was cool to see how things come together behind the scenes. I've always had strong facial expressions and features, even as a baby, so that just helps make it more interesting, I guess. On the nerd scene, the Duffers didn't tell me what to do with my facial expressions, or voice, or anything. I was just in character. With the syrup scene, the script didn't have Erica say "Sorry" at the end... on the walkie-talkie scene, "Like I said" wasn't in the script either. Those things just felt right at the time, while playing Erica, so I did it and the Duffers decided to keep it in there, which was really cool. I don't think too much. I prepare, but I do what feels good in my heart."

(586) Pyramid Head, one of the monsters in Silent Hill, was an inspiration for the Demogorgon. Both are monsters without a face.

(587) In the arcade scenes in Stranger Things 2 you can see the games Asteroids, Galaga and Pac-Man in the background.

(588) Linnea Berthelsen said she'd never seen Stranger Things when she was asked to audition for it and so stayed up until 4 in the morning binge watching the first season.

(589) Dungeons & Dragons fans have suggested that the Mind Flayer might be a aboleth. Aboleths are tentacled monsters with psionic powers. In a Dungeons & Dragons magazine they were described this way - "In general, all aboleth are cruel, emotionless, and logical. All are extremely intelligent — some even more so than the most ancient of elven mages. They are believed to live for thousands of years, but exact information is difficult to gain. Over their many years of existence, the aboleth have developed a society which far exceeds that of humans in efficiency. In this society, each aboleth has a specific duty which it performs with the utmost skill. There are four major roles in the aboleth society. In increasing order of importance, these roles are: slave gathering, slave maintenance, scientific research and experimentation, and ruling. An aboleth feeds mainly on microscopic organisms which abound in its natural habitat, but it can also consume larger prey if necessary. Aboleth can survive in both air and water, but prefer water for obvious reasons. It is worthy to note that rumours exist of a grand aboleth, a creature so immense that it dwarfs even the rulers. If so, then perhaps it is better that surface and subterranean dwellers alike leave the aboleth to do as they please."

(590) The art of Polish painter Zdzislaw Beksinski was an influence on the look of the Upside Down.

(591) The M9s that some of the agents carry in Stranger Things did not become a U.S military sidearm until 1985.

(592) Hopper's knife in season one seems too modern for 1983. It has half-serrated folders with thumb studs.

(593) Millie Bobby Brown says she was amazed Eleven

became so popular. She thought Eleven was going to be a "sidekick".

(594) Unlike little Erica, Priah Ferguson is not a big fan of syrup. "I'm not a big breakfast person, to be honest. I'm not a big…I like lunch and dinner because I feel like there are more options. But my mom and my sister, they're all about syrup, they love syrup. But I'm not a big, sweet, breakfast person. I don't know. I'm not a big fan of syrup. Now, I'll eat it on pancakes if my mom tells me to eat breakfast, because I really, I really don't eat breakfast in the morning. Sometimes, but she'll say, "Breakfast is healthy for you!" It's not my favourite thing in the world. I like oatmeal."

(595) Dee Wallace, one of the stars of E.T. The Extra-Terrestrial, says she would love to be in Stranger Things. "I want to be on it! It has style, and they have been able to capture the eighties with today's spin so that it is very relevant."

(596) Aaron Sims says the early concept art depicting the death of Barb at the hands of the Demogorgon was more grisly and graphic than what eventually ended up on the screen. "Based on our original discussion with the Duffers on this design, we wanted to go really graphic with it to highlight the horrific aspects of Barb being eaten, and something then growing on top of her - thus, the ribs poking out of her stomach in the first shot. In the final design, they ended up veering away from that because it became too unrecognizable. It was difficult to tell exactly what had happened to her; it wasn't an issue of it being too graphic, but rather, that the viewer needed to see something that was very recognizably dead. In the script for that episode, there was specifically a description of a spider coming out of her mouth, which we incorporated into the design of that second shot ... we don't really have an explanation for its existence; the design is based around the script's description."

(597) The budget for the first season was $6 million an episode.

(598) Will, Eleven and Sara Hopper are all seen with what seems to be a similar stuffed Lion toy at various stages in Stranger Things.

(599) The song that plays during Will's funeral in season one is Elegia by New Order.

(600) Ross Duffer was amused by the DOE releasing a statement when Stranger Things came out! "I love that the Department of Energy issued a public statement that they're not evil. That's my favourite thing."

(601) Matt Duffer says Stranger Things is more about suspense than gore. "There are a few small instances where we pulled back on the violence. But, even when you talk about a movie like Halloween, these are movies that are much more about mood and atmosphere and suspense and dread than they are about gore. That was what we were more interested in: the dread and eeriness. So we didn't feel like we had to restrain ourselves in this instance to the TV-14 rating area. We basically wrote whatever we wanted."

(602) Caleb McLaughlin had to audition five times before he got the part of Lucas.

(603) In the first episode of season two, Mike calls Eleven at 7:40 p.m. 7 + 4 = 11.

(604) David Harbour, who is old enough to remember the eighties, says that Stranger Things makes the decade seem better than it actually was.

(605) Ross Duffer says that he and Matt related to the

character of Barb. "For us it's easy to relate to her because high school was terrible for us and I know it was for a lot of people. You either love it or hate it, and we hated it. And so I think there's a lot of people that feel like they were on the outside looking in, like Barb. All I know is it was very easy for us to write the Barb character and I think that, you know, Shannon Purser — who had never acted before — just did such a brilliant job realizing her. And, again, without very many lines — 25 lines. And I think everyone feels like either they knew this girl or they were this girl."

(606) In Numerology, "Eleven symbolizes the potential to push the limitations of the human experience into the stratosphere of the highest spiritual perception; the link between the mortal and the immortal; between man and spirit; between darkness and light; ignorance and enlightenment."

(607) The blue/white flashlight beams in Stranger Things season one are not correct for the era. Flashlights from this era had an orange/yellow glow.

(608) The families of the cast members were not allowed to read the Stranger Things 2 scripts. "My brother always asks me to send him the texts," said Gaten Matazarro. "I had to answer him that the conditions were much stricter this season. We did not want copies to reach hackers."

(609) Will is the only one of the boys in Stranger Things who doesn't seem to swear from time to time.

(610) The Duffers say that they always had a nostalgic feeling for the eighties and a time when technology wasn't quite as ubiquitous as it is today. "We have vague memories of the Eighties, but we were still pre-Internet and pre–cell phone for most of our childhood. We were the last generation to have the experience of going out with our friends to the woods or

the train tracks and the only way our parents could connect with us was to say, 'It's time for dinner.' We were also movie nerds and had all these VHS tapes of all these classic Eighties films that we would watch over and over again. That was our point of reference for what it was like in the late Seventies and early Eighties."

(611) The police light-bar on the Chief Hopper's 1980 Blazer is a Code 3 MX7000. This was not sold until the 1990s.

(612) Amy Seimetz, who plays Becky Ives, is a director in addition to being an actor and directed on the second season of The Girlfriend Experience.

(613) When she heard the story for season one, Millie Bobby Brown asked why the Byers family didn't just telephone Will to see where he was. They had to explain to her that cell phones didn't exist in the 1980s.

(614) Amy Seimetz, like Winona Ryder and Paul Reiser, has appeared in an Alien film. She was in Alien: Covenant.

(615) Casting director Carmen Cuba says when casting kids that - "Training and/or life experience teaches adults how to leave some of their quirks off the table. But kids are mostly unable to cover up the things that make them uniquely who they are — and I love that."

(616) Matt Duffer says they loved the idea of scaring children with Stranger Things - just as they had been scared by movies they watched as kids. "When we were growing up, some of those Amblin films, those Spielberg movies, led to the creation of the PG-13 rating because he was pushing it so dark and he upset a lot of parents. I liked that, though. I think that that's good and healthy and great and some of our favourite experiences growing up were having the shit scared out of us. As we get further into the show, especially when you get into

the final episode, it ratchets up a notch. But by then you've already got the kids watching, so then we can scare the s*** out of them. Then the parents can get mad."

(617) In season two, Hopper promises Eleven he'll be home at 5:15. 5 + 1 + 5 = 11.

(618) Unlike the Duffers, Sean Astin says he sort of understands why some people thought that Bob might turn out to be a baddie. "I guess I see that. I stepped into the role when they hadn't 100 percent decided what they were going to do with Bob, so I guess that possibility could have happened. Who could possibly be that nice, right? But I think Bob serves a function for the show in that he's the one person in Hawkins who isn't in the middle of all that stuff. It's flattering that you're glad I didn't turn evil because the other option is that I could have turned bad and lived! Would I rather be alive and bad or dead and heroic? I think it went down exactly as I would have liked."

(619) Caleb McLaughlin says he became an actor because of his sister. "My sister actually introduced me to acting. We went to this community theatre in our town called Pied Piper and she didn't wanna do it by herself. I was 7, but I didn't professionally do it until I was 10."

(620) On the first take of the scene where Eleven flips the van over the bicycles, one of the explosives failed and the van ended up destroying an expensive camera.

(621) The bus Eleven takes to Chicago to see Kali/Eight is the 422. 4 + 2 + 2 = 8.

(622) Shawn Levy says they consulted with the Game of Thrones team to learn how to keep the plot of Stranger Things 2 a secret during production. "Literally one of our producers consulted with the Game of Thrones producers to learn about

their security protocols. Because suddenly we were just this little show by two twin brothers [The Duffer Brothers] and a film director and we're like, we think it's cool, but we don't know if anyone's going to watch it. And now we're this thing that the world is paying attention to, and so we definitely had to be a little more careful with our creative secrets."

(623) The Duffers say that the fact the children are growing up fast is good because it means Stranger Things will feel different each time it returns. "It forces the show to evolve and change, because the kids are changing. Even if we wanted it to be static and we wanted to continually recycle the same storyline — and we don't — we would be unable to, just because the kids are changing. It's cool, though. The audience is going to be able to watch these kids come of age every year. The closest example is Harry Potter. Watching those kids and actors grow up in front of the camera was, to me, very powerful."

(624) Natalia Dyer says she had no idea how Stranger Things season one was going to end because the Duffers were still writing the last episodes while they were shooting the early ones.

(625) Gaten Matarazzo says that he does what he does not because he loves red carpets but because he loves acting. He can take or leave the fame but acting is the passion.

(626) The Duffers thought about making Stranger Things a film at first but quickly decided that a TV series would be better with the longer format.

(627) When they were in the third grade the Duffers made a film based on trading card game Magic: The Gathering.

(628) When Bob is dressed as Dracula on Halloween night this feels like a joke reference to the fact that Winona Ryder was in

Francis Ford Coppola's Dracula movie.

(629) Millie Bobby Brown came up with Eleven's 'laser beam stare'. "I've never forgotten it, because it was so intuitive," said executive producer Shawn Levy. "That this little person had such fierce power — that's what took me aback. That same day the Duffers [brothers Matt and Ross, who created the show] and I knew she was the one."

(630) Dacre Montgomery said he gained some weight and lost the 'ripped' muscles he had for the Power Rangers movie to play Billy because it didn't think it was realistic for an early eighties teenager to look too 'super-shredded'.

(631) Millie Bobby Brown, as of 2018, is said to be worth $3 million. Not bad for a 14 year-old.

(632) Given the stage background of many members of the younger cast and the musical inclinations of the others, the makeup artist on Stranger Things says there is a lot of singing going on when the kids are on set.

(633) When listening to the Stranger Things theme song on Spotify, the album cover page turns into the upside down.

(634) Ross Duffer said the chapter titles at the start of each episode are designed to make the viewer feel as if they are reading a book. "It's exciting that this is Netflix and not a movie, and that's why we put the chapter title cards on every episode. We wanted it to feel like you're sitting down and reading this big fat Stephen King book."

(635) Dustin's totally tubular catchphrase with Max might be a reference to the film Hocus Pocus.

(636) Natalia Dyer thinks the eighties seems like a fun and innocent era compared to today. "Very different from our

current information overload."

(637) Finn Wolfhard would like to be a director one day and feels as if he learned a lot from the Duffers working on Stranger Things. "What I've learned from them - and I have learned a lot from Shawn Levy, too - is to be confident in my choices and vision and to make sure you have the best people around you who will execute those choices in the service of the vision. Leaving room for improv and unplanned moments is also really valuable because a good idea can come from anywhere. The Duffers are also incredibly patient and trusting in both their cast and their crew, and that gives everyone else involved the confidence to do their best work and be fearless. It's really a virtuous circle that comes right back to the director."

(638) Winona Ryder was convicted of grand theft, shoplifting, and vandalism after appearing to shoplift designer items from a Beverly Hills department store in 2001. She was sentenced to three years' probation and 480 hours of community service. Winona said that strong painkilling medication had affected her state of mind at the time.

(639) The Lovecraft story which has the most similarities with Stranger Things is From Beyond. The book was published in 1920 and is about dark secret dimensions unknown to man.

(640) Cade Jones, who plays the bully James in season one, says that like Peyton Wich, he got on great in real life with the kids his character had to be mean to onscreen.

(641) The school bullies Troy and James were absent from season two. Might they return in the future? We'll have to see.

(642) Stranger Things has some similarities to Paper Girls, a comic by Brian K Vaughan which started in 2015. Paper Girls is set in the late 1980s and revolves around four young girls

who get mixed up in inter-dimensional time travel.

(643) The scene in season one where Mike pretends to be ill so that he can skip school and spend the day with Eleven is a reference to Ferris Bueller's Day Off.

(644) Ross Duffer says of the final shot in season two that - "They've shut the door on the Mind Flayer, but not only is it still there in the Upside Down, it's very much aware of the kids, and particularly Eleven. It had not encountered her and her powers until that final episode. Now, it knows that she's out there. We wanted to end on a little bit of an ominous note."

(645) Special effects expert Paul Graf says of the Demodogs that - "When they come out of the hole, and we first see them walk somewhere, they have both a human-like way of moving and a dog-like way of moving and a raptor-like way of moving, so definitely 'Jurassic Park' for a lot of the scenes was somewhere there in our minds."

(646) Dart was time consuming to design because he had to go through four stages of development from slug to Deomodog.

(647) Millie Bobby Brown says her perfect snack is hummus and carrots.

(648) The Duffers say that some of the flower/flesh qualities of the Demogorgon were inspired by the 1978 remake film Invasion of the Body Snatchers.

(649) Millie Bobby Brown says that when she's in England she loves waking up to watch This Morning and Loose Women - two magazine shows that would probably be regarded as guilty pleasures.

(650) Noah Schnapp says he has never been on Facebook and

calls it social media for old people!

(651) Caleb McLaughlin, Gaten Matarazzo, and Millie Bobby Brown have all said they are fans of The Walking Dead when asked to name other shows (besides Stranger Things) that they watch.

(652) Gaten Matarazzo says that when it comes to music he likes Green Day and Pearl Jam, Led Zeppelin, Rush, My Chemical Romance, and Foo Fighters.

(653) Caleb McLaughlin says he plays video games when there is a lull on the set of Stranger Things. "I do definitely take my games, because when it's a rainy day, what do you do? Do you just look at the sky? Of course, you read a book, because that helps you in life. But you play your video games."

(654) Caleb says the three games he loves the most are GTA V, NBA 2K, and Destiny.

(655) The success of Stranger Things and The Walking Dead as Georgia based productions has seen Atlanta dubbed 'Hollywood East'.

(656) One reason why so many shows and films are shooting in Georgia besides the competitive tax advantages is that the area has distinct seasons and a range of landscapes from small towns to forests to rocky terrains. It can be made to look like anywhere.

(657) Stranger Things is coloured by Skip Kimball at Technicolor.

(658) Matt Duffer says that they weren't completely sure whether or not the bike chase in season one was a great idea but gave in to their instincts. "The bike chase, it felt very

organic to the story that there would be a bike chase. But of course, we were like, "Is this a bad idea? Crossing a line? We can't do a bike chase." It's just so E.T., obviously. In that instance, I think we just gave into our weaker impulses and wrote the bike chase, and it's out of our system. So we don't ever have to do it again."

(659) Matt Duffer says that the thing they loved about Netflix is that they didn't have to stipulate a specific number of episodes would be made. They could choose how long or short Stranger Things would be. "We didn't know how to make the story 13 episodes. I feel like it starts to tread water. It was important, and it felt like a movie, and in order for it to feel like a movie, we had to keep it on the shorter side. Even if there is a season 2, I think we keep the number down again. Otherwise, I think it starts to lose that more cinematic feel."

(660) It wasn't just eighties props that were needed in Stranger Things but also 1970s pieces according to Chris Trujillo. "A lot of that is approached from understanding the characters on a socioeconomic level. You've got your stressed out, working class, single mom [character], so her house is not going to have the most up-to-date furniture from 1980 or '81. For that kind of set, we like to think about when that furniture would have been bought and what level of wear and tear it would have. And understanding that more than likely, she hasn't redecorated since 1975."

(661) Why doesn't Karen Wheeler ever check the basement in season one? Matt Duffer - "She's happily oblivious. She has no reason to think anything. My mindset is, when we were growing up, and we were making these really bad nerdy movies, we would just wander off. We were left alone all day. They didn't come into our world. We didn't want our parents coming into our world. To me, Mike and his friends spend an obscene amount of time in his basement playing these never ending Dungeons and Dragons campaigns. Karen just doesn't

come down there. She has no reason to be concerned."

(662) Chris Trujillo says that it was important not to make the eighties trappings of Stranger Things too on the nose. "It's particularly tricky with the '80s because everybody has a very specific and sometimes outlandish sense of what the '80s look like. It's all either neons or these big shoulder pads and big glasses. And obviously you need to show those things but it was definitely tricky to find a balance where you're not distracting an audience by blasting them with the most obvious touchstones of what we think of when we think of the '80s. Firstly, we try and understand who these characters are on a really basic level and we kind of go from there."

(663) The Duffers say the failure of their film Hidden was a big factor in them turning their attention to television. "Yeah, it was unbelievable to us at the time, and then that ended up going from a dream experience to crashing and burning. We didn't know what the hell else we were going to do with our lives, this is all we knew how to do. We felt like we'd been preparing to do this since we were little kids. Looking back on it, for us, it was using that low point as an advantage. I don't think Stranger Things would exist without it, because it was us being disillusioned with movies, the things we fell in love with, and then seeing this other opening in television that, if we really want to tell the kind of stories we want to tell, maybe we were just looking in the wrong place."

(664) Shawn Levy thinks that audiences connect with the eighties nostalgia in Stranger Things because it was - in his opinion - a better time. "The world felt safer. The world, and it breaks my heart to say this, but the world was safer. And I know that a lot of us yearn for the relative innocence of that. And I do think that the show transports us back to a cultural and global climate that was fundamentally more comforting. It was fundamentally less scary."

(665) The Duffers say they weren't very social in high school and used to each lunch together in their car rather than the canteen.

(666) Shawn Levy says he knew Gaten Matarazzo should be in the show the moment he first met him. "The second Gaten walked in, we were like, Okay well we're done looking for Dustin, because he's in the room with us right frickin' now. I remember that being the most un-debatable casting decision. He has the greatest face on planet Earth, and he has such a natural comedic instinct that we needed in that group. We knew Mike was going to be something of a leader. We knew Lucas was dealing with suspicion and anger. So we needed a force of pure positivity and levity, and Gaten walked in with that."

(667) In season one, Hopper has to search through a swathe of microfiche in the library to research the Hawkins Lab. Microfiche is a flat piece of film containing microphotographs of the pages of a newspaper, catalogue, or other document.

(668) Some fans saw references to the 1985 film D.A.R.Y.L. in Stranger Things. D.A.R.Y.L. is about a young boy with no memory or home who is taken in by a family and turns out be an artificial intelligence experiment wanted by the authorities. The Duffers denied this particular reference though and said they had never heard of D.A.R.Y.L.

(669) Millie Bobby Brown says that when she gets home from the Stranger Things set she loves instant ramen noodles because you don't have to wait around before you can eat something.

(670) A DVD release of season one by Target was designed so that the DVD case looked like a faded VHS tape.

(671) You can now buy Stranger Things action figures,

Stranger Things toy cars, and Stranger Things Monopoly.

(672) You can even buy a (somewhat weird it has to be said) Eleven candle holder that makes her bleed from the nose as the candle wax melts. The blurb was this - "After a series of harrowing experiments in a shady forest laboratory... we finally managed to make this ornament bleed from the nose. The Eleven Bleeding Nose Candle is easily the strangest thing we've ever created. Simply melt the red candle inside this hefty ceramic bust, and 'blood' will trickle out of her nostrils – just like she's overexerted herself during a psychokinetic episode. Depending on her mood; other abilities may include – crushing coke cans, making bullies wet themselves and generally warding off creatures from the upside-down. This giant ornament comes with two red candles and we've even included a handy 'nose picker' tool in case she gets a blockage."

(673) Other Stranger Things merchandise includes a Steve Harrington Babysitter's Club bag and an Eggo card game!

(674) Paul Reiser says it was hard to make Owens seem sincere in his first scene where he's trying to get Will's trust. "I remember the first scene I shot, where I implore David [Harbour] and Winona [Ryder] to trust me, and no matter how hard I tried, I just sounded so full of s***. I'm like, "You know what, I don't trust me!" I couldn't find a way to not seem like just the worst guy in the world, and it was a fun way to start."

(675) Gaten Matarazzo fundraises for CCD Smiles, an organization that provides financial assistance to those who require treatment for cleidocranial dysplasia.

(676) David Harbour says he likes superheroes that don't have special powers, like Batman.

(677) In the very early plans for Stranger Things 2, Bob Newby was only going to appear in one episode.

(678) Shawn Levy says he is still surprised by the amount of people who refuse to accept that Barb is really dead. "I'll give one example that I've been asked about a hundred times which is people still think Barb's alive. Because you think you want that, but you wouldn't really want that. I've had a lot of people, some huge celebrities come up to me at these awards shows, like, 'So, between us, Barb's coming back, right?' I'm like 'No, you saw, she had like a creature, slug, worm, snake, coming out of her mouth. I don't know that there's a bounce back from that!'"

(679) It took about five months to film the first season of Stranger Things.

(680) Sadie Sink says that - "I was so superstitious during my auditions for Stranger Things that after each audition I would put each audition scene on the car floor and refused to pick them up until after the process was over!"

(681) IT director Andy Muschietti says he had never heard of Stranger Things when he cast Finn Wolfhard in his film. "I had no idea what Stranger Things was, in fact. Stranger Things came out in the middle of production. We were probably halfway through the shoot, or something, before Stranger Things came out. In fact, I picked Finn in the cast without knowing that he was in that show. But once it came out, people immediately... you know, it was a hit. So everyone started talking about it. And I didn't want to see it. I didn't want to watch it. It wasn't until post-production... after the shoot, it took me like two months to actually watch an episode. It's great. It's very cool. It's very good."

(682) Millie Bobby Brown trains in Thai boxing and ju-jitsu.

(683) Winona Ryder is estimated to be worth $18 million.

(684) The twilight realm in the video game Zelda was an influence on the Upside Down.

(685) Eleven's blonde wig in season one cost $8,000.

(686) Ross Duffer says that Barb was discussed a lot in the writer discussions for season one despite only featuring in a couple of episodes. "We were always talking about Barb and 'what about Barb' and 'poor Barb' — we talked about it in the writers' room almost every day…. there's something particularly tragic about the loner character getting snatched and not making it out of the Upside Down."

(687) Observers of a scientific bent were impressed by the kiddie pool sensory deprivation tank scene. It seemed legit to most of them.

(688) The first modern day sensory float tank was invented in the 1970s.

(689) The entry to the afterparty for Stranger Things 2 was fashioned after the Hawkins Town Fair.

(690) In early scripts for season one, Jonathan worked in a cinema. "Jonathan had a job at the movie theatre, and so he and Nancy used that movie theater in Hawkins as their hideout once they were aware of the monster," said Shawn Levy.

(691) Paul Reiser and Sean Astin are the wealthiest cast members Stranger Things has had. Both are said to be worth $40 million.

(692) Joe Keery says he understood that Steve was going to be a school swimming star when he was first cast but in the end

this was abandoned and we didn't get to see Steve in the pool. "At the beginning of the first season, I got the part and talked to the Duffer brothers [show creators], and they were saying, 'He's going to be kinda like this jock character and he's, like, a swimmer.' So for the first, I don't know, six weeks prior to shooting, I was training, doing all this swimming prep."

(693) Netflix members voted Stranger Things as the top show that could be watched as a family.

(694) Regarding the sensory deprivation tank scene in the lab, Millie Bobby Brown says it is very difficult to scream while in underwater apparatus!

(695) The Duffers say they are more scared of science based horror than spiritual horror. In other words, the thought of aliens or secret government experiments are more frightening to them than ghosts.

(696) Bob was going to spew a torrent of blood from his mouth when he was killed by Demodogs but the Duffers decided this was too gruesome for Stranger Things and negated the blood and gore of Bob's death.

(697) Set dresser Craig Johnson says that during the lunch break for the arcade scenes in Stranger Things 2 they were allowed to play the arcade games and they all worked.

(698) The moment where Barb spits out a mouthful of goo in the Upside Down swimming pool required fourteen takes.

(699) The edible goo mixture had to be syringed into Shannon Purser's mouth before each take.

(700) "She's literally covered in the disgusting, slimy material that coats the other dimension in our show and hanging off a pool railing with me and a bunch of stunt guys yanking at her

ankles to simulate the monster dragging her to oblivion," said Shawn Levy of Shannon Purser during Barb's death scene.

(701) Joe Keery says one of the most difficult things about playing Steve is the super tight jeans he has to wear! "It felt like Bruce Springsteen jeans or something like that. I don't know if you could tell, but the entire railroad track scene, I'm bunching at the crotch extremely. They're like Dennis Quaid in Breaking Away sort of jeans. But you know, I think it's the style for the time period. It was pretty funny."

(702) In the employee room of the Palace Arcade you can see posters for Q*bert and Crystal Castles.

(703) The name of the Palace Arcade was taken from WarGames.

(704) The building transformed into the arcade was a complete mess before the production designers transformed it according to Matt Duffer. "I don't know what [the building] was [before]. It was disgusting, whatever it was. I mean, there was so much junk in there. You could not move without falling over. I didn't go in there because it was unhealthy."

(705) The Duffers say that locals in Georgia were disappointed when they learned this wasn't a real arcade that was opening for the public!

(706) The Duffers say they played Pac-Man in the arcade when they had some spare time on the set.

(707) The arcade scenes foreshadow the rest of the season. Ross Duffer - "We were hoping to do with the arcade what we did in season one with D&D, which was to do a bit of foreshadowing for the whole season, with Lucas getting Princess Daphne, and the monsters in Dig-Dug. We were hoping to roughly set up where we were going to go in the

next nine hours."

(708) The girls admiring Billy's posterior at the start of Stranger Things 2 are sitting against a Mustang which wasn't issued until 1986.

(709) Matt Duffer says the idea of Will experiencing an Upside Down vision outside the arcade was an early powerful image that helped to shape season two. "We're starting work on season three, and you start to get excited about different imagery [when you start a season]. So we had an idea of an arcade, of him seeing a storm outside of the arcade, that helped define the season for us."

(710) When we see Bob and Joyce kissing in the store in Stranger Things 2 you can see an Annie wig. This is a probable reference to the fact that Sadie Sink played Annie on the stage.

(711) Joe Keery says it was tough to shoot the party scene in Stranger Things 2 where a drunk Nancy tells Steve she doesn't love him. "I had never really done a scene where I had to be as emotionally available. It's just a hard thing to stay in — to stay in this limbo of doing the scene and then talking to crew members while they're eating turkey sandwiches and then go back and get your heart broken again. It's a really tough part about the job that I think even I didn't fully understand."

(712) Finn Wolfhard ate tic tacs before the scene where he has to kiss Eleven in the first season finale.

(713) The articles on the Police Station bulletin board in the first season finale are - The Boy Who Came Back To Life, Hawkins Lab Blocks Inquiry, More Heads Roll in Ongoing State Trooper Scandal, and Coroner Arrested for Falsifying Autopsy.

(714) The Bathtub is the first episode of Stranger Things that

takes place on the same day.

(715) Winona Ryder says that when she lived in a commune as a child with no electricity they sometimes used to watch old movies projected onto a barn.

(716) Matt Duffer says he doesn't like the game Dragon's Lair very much. "Dragon's Lair we played a lot as kids. It's a fun game to look at — it's not a very fun game to play. Everyone who played it as a kid had the same experience: It's outrageously expensive, it looks really cool, it draws you in like a magnet, and then it just takes your money and is very frustrating. All these barcades are popping up now, and I was at one recently and they had Dragon's Lair there. And no one is playing it because it's not a very good game. But it's still 50 cents! It's 2017 now, and 50 cents is a lot less, but it still felt like it was ripping you off. It's such an impossible game."

(717) The song played at the beginning of The Body is Atmosphere by Joy Division.

(718) In season one you can see houses that don't have TV antennas. This is an anachronism for 1983.

(719) The Duffers say the 'Justice for Barb' subplot in season two ending up being longer and more substantial than they'd originally planned.

(720) The photographs of Barb as a child that Nancy sobs over in the bathroom of the Holland family are real childhood photographs of Shannon Purser.

(721) Millie Bobby Brown has 12 million Instagram followers.

(722) When Mr Clarke is watching John Carpenter's The Thing at home with his date he explains that the head stretching effects were done with bubblegum. Old school special effects

indeed!

(723) The music during the construction of the home-made sensory deprivation tank in The Bathtub is Fields of Coral from the 1996 album Oceanic by Vangelis.

(724) In the second episode of Stranger Things 2, Dustin wears a Casio F-91W digital watch. These were only available from 1991.

(725) Gaten Matarazzo had an injured ankle during shooting of the first season finale but still managed to carry Millie Bobby Brown in the scene where Dustin carries the exhausted Eleven into the classroom.

(726) Dustin is wearing a Castroville Artichoke Festival t-shirt in the last two episodes of season one.

(727) In the last episode of season one, the boys play Dungeons & Dragons and muse on how short the campaign was. This is a meta reference to the fact that Stranger Things 1 only consisted of eight episodes.

(728) Dustin wears Ghostbusters sneakers to the Snow Ball dance.

(729) In Stranger Things 2, Max has a poster for the 1966 surf movie The Endless Summer in her room.

(730) When Eleven breaks through the wall in the second episode of season two to escape from the Upside Down, she enters our world again at the same point in the wall that the Demogorgon used when it crashed into the school.

(731) The hazmat suits in season one sometimes have LED lights with a hue that didn't exist in 1983.

(732) Bob choosing to watch Mr Mom at Halloween is an in-joke as Winona Ryder famously featured with Mr Mom star Michael Keaton in Tim Burton's Beetlejuice.

(733) The passage from Anne of Green Gables that Hopper reads to Eleven in the cabin is this - "I would feel so sad if I was a disappointment to her — because she didn't live very long after that, you see. She died of a fever when I was just three months old. I do wish she'd lived long enough for me to remember calling her mother. I think it would be so sweet to say 'mother,' don't you? And father died four days afterwards from fever too. That left me an orphan and folks were at their wits' end, so Mrs. Thomas said, what to do with me. You see, nobody wanted me even then. It seems to be my fate."

(734) When Steve and Nancy are musing over Steve's college essay in Stranger Things 2 they actually had a real essay which someone had written for the scene.

(735) When Hopper and Owens meet at the end of season two in the diner this is a sly reference to the cult 1982 film Diner which Paul Reiser acted in.

(736) When Mike is throwing some toys away in Stranger Things 2 we see he has a Teenage Mutant Ninja Turtle action figure but these weren't released until 1988.

(737) Elle (El) is a famous character in Silent Hill: Homecoming.

(738) The Duffers say they couldn't resist the idea of a car chase to start season two. "Matt and I have just always wanted to do a car chase, so that was the impetus, just to do a car chase. It was very fun to shoot."

(739) The radio at the cabin that Eleven and Hopper use to communicate in Stranger Things 2 is set on broadcast channel

11.

(740) In the episode The Pollywog you can see a Buzz Lightyear doll in Dustin's room. This is a mistake as Toy Story wasn't released until 1995.

(741) The Peterbilt truck in Dig Dug is a reference to the episode's director Andrew Stanton's Pixar film Cars.

(742) In Stranger Things 2, Family Feud is playing in Terry Ives house. The host of the quiz show is Richard Dawson. There is a Stephen King connection here as Dawson played the sinister game show host Damon Killian in the 1987 film adaptation of Stephen King's story The Running Man.

(743) When Mike pauses and looks reflective when he picks up the dinosaur while clearing out his old toys for a yard sale in MADMAX, this is because the dinosaur was one of the first things he showed Eleven in season one when she lived in his basement.

(744) Ross Duffer says Dacre Montgomery's audition was the most "bonkers" he has ever seen. "It was great. It had that kind of edge and energy you needed for Billy. This is a guy who can be fun one second, and in the next, you're terrified for your life."

(745) The Duffers say that the casting of Sean Astin had a big effect on season two. "I think of all the people that we cast, he shaped the season and the course of the character more than anyone else. When we started writing for him, we just really enjoyed it and we wanted him in more and more scenes. It just really changed the direction of the whole season."

(746) When Jonathan is in the woods outside Steve's house with his camera in Stranger Things season one, this is a homage to Brian De Palma's film Body Double.

(747) The lead hairdresser, Sarah Hindsgaul, based Eleven's curls on the cover of Swedish author Astrid Lindgren's 1981 book Ronja Rövardotter, which depicts a nomadic young girl with dishevelled hair. "She's wild, she's free, she's ungroomed. That's what we need for Eleven — somebody who's not aware of self yet."

(748) Joe Keery says he still had a job waiting tables when he was told he had the part of Steve.

(749) The orange cat who hisses at Eleven in season one might be a reference to the ginger cat in Ridley Scott's Alien.

(750) The Duffers say that a number of storylines they couldn't find room for in Stranger Things 2 will probably be used for Stranger Things 3.

(751) IMDB users rate The Gate as the best episode of Stranger Things and The Lost Sister as the worst.

(752) The car chase scene which starts in Stranger Things 2 was shot in Atlanta with the Pittsburgh skyline added in later.

(753) They couldn't find a large tunnel in Atlanta for the car chase and so had to extend one with CGI according to Matt Duffer. "You just cannot find a bridge anywhere even near Atlanta. You actually can't even find a tunnel. That tunnel was actually about 20 feet long. It was ridiculous. It was the tiniest, puniest tunnel, and we just ended up extending it with computer graphics."

(754) Millie Bobby Brown was - appropriately enough - eleven years-old during the production of season one.

(755) Matt Duffer says the Duffers love of Gremlins was the obvious source of the Dustin/Dart story. "I love Gremlins. I

also love Gremlins 2. I think it's just a really great series. Aside from Will being possessed, that story line was always baked into our first idea: a boy and his monster, Dustin finding a creature that will grow."

(756) In the second season, Jonathan picks up a Polaroid cartridge with the words Impossible Impulse Battery visible. This company reference for Polaroid film wasn't founded until 2007.

(757) Winona Ryder was born in 1971 and so in 1983 would have been more or less the same age as the kids were meant to be in season one.

(758) One of the Stranger Things camera assistants - Clyde Bryan - shot the scene where Mr Clarke is watching John Carpenter's The Thing at home and also worked on that very same movie.

(759) Linnea Berthelsen says it was fun to become a punk. "It was a really great creative process and it was a lot of fun to see how the costume designer and hair designer developed the characters. I remember the first day we did a small screen test with the whole crew, and we had the van, and they took some pictures. That was the first time we saw the gang together and it was terrifying, because we'd only seen everyone without their makeup on."

(760) Gamezebo said this of the Stranger Things computer game - "A game that is both a fantastic expansion of the Stranger Things universe as well as an homage to video games of the '80s and '90s. While The Legend of Zelda is the most strongly represented series, there are nostalgic details throughout from a Super Mario star on the police station to a reference to the E.T.: the Extra-Terrestrial game in the local dump. Little touches, like different dialogues from NPCs depending on who you have selected as your active character,

bring the world to life and reward players who explore in depth. The amount of game here—easily six hours plus—is massive for an app that is 100% free without ads or in-app purchases, with each of those hours lovingly crafted by a team that obviously cares about all of its source material. This is a gift to fans of Stranger Things or NES/SNES-era adventures with no strings attached, except the time you'll inevitably lose once you're sucked into its world."

(761) The character of Kali was originally going to be called Roman.

(762) Shannon Purser says she was a huge Winona Ryder fan even before Stranger Things came along. "I've been a huge Winona Ryder fan for a while. I'm one of four girls, so there are four sisters, so we used to watch Little Women seriously, maybe once a month. From a pretty young age, I really loved Winona and the kind of characters she played. I think she's just incredible. Even just seeing her around, because I didn't really have scenes with her, I was in major freak-out mode."

(763) Dacre Montgomery says his under the leg basketball dunk in Stranger Things 2 was a lucky fluke.

(764) Good Housekeeping said that babies given the name Dustin were up by 32% in the year after Stranger Things was released!

(765) The Duffers say they play music when they write the Stranger Things scripts. Two scores they love playing when writing are the soundtracks to The Dark Knight and The Matrix.

(766) Millie Bobby Brown was only told she would have to cut her hair for the part of Eleven after the final audition.

(767) David Harbour's acceptance speech at the The Screen

Actors Guild (SAG) when Stranger Things won the award for outstanding performance in an ensemble in a drama series is near legendary - not least for the baffled reactions of Winona Ryder. This was Harbour's speech - "I would just like to say that in light of everything that's going on in the world today, it's difficult to celebrate the already celebrated Stranger Things, but this award from you who take your craft seriously and earnestly believe, like me, that great acting can change the world, is a call to arms from our fellow craftsmen and women to go deeper, and through our art to battle against fear, self-centredness, and exclusivity of our predominately narcissistic culture, and through our craft to cultivate a more empathetic and understanding society by revealing intimate truths that serve as a forceful reminder to folks that when they feel broken and afraid and tired, they are not alone.

We are united in that we are all human beings and we are all together on this horrible, painful, joyous, exciting, and mysterious ride that is being alive. Now, as we act in the continuing narrative of Stranger Things, we 1983 midwesterners will repel bullies. We will shelter freaks and outcasts — those who have no hope. We will get past the lies. We will hunt monsters. When we are at a loss amidst the hypocrisy and casual violence of certain individuals and institutions, we will, as per Chief Jim Hopper, punch some people in the face when they seek to destroy the meek and the disenfranchised and the marginalized. And we will do it all with soul, with heart, and with joy. We thank you for this responsibility."

(768) A promo poster posted on Stranger Thing's social media accounts to promote the show was based on the poster for Ridley Scott's Alien.

(769) Other famous films which were used as the basis for Stranger Things promo posters included Firestarter and The Evil Dead.

(770) In the very first episode of Stranger Things, Ted Wheeler is struggling to get a good TV reception. The show he is trying to watch is Knight Rider with David Hasselhoff.

(771) The Duffers say that when they casting the part of Max they made the initial mistake of auditioning girls who were a little too young. "Initially, we made the mistake of [acting] like we were casting season one. So the girls we picked out, we started to read them across from our boys and [the girls] were just little. They were too young. We forgot that our boys had aged a year."

(772) When Millie Bobby Brown appeared on breakfast television in Britain after Stranger Things came out, viewers were amazed to discover that she was British in real life because her American accent in Stranger Things had been so convincing.

(773) We see a brief snippet of the classic sitcom Cheers when Eleven is watching television in the cabin in Stranger Things 2.

(774) David Harbour says that Hopper wearing Sara's hair bracelet has this meaning - "I'll fiddle with it, almost like you would with a wedding ring when you're going through a divorce but you're still wearing it. It's a constant reminder to him of his struggles and his guilt around not being about to save his child."

(775) In the last quarter of 2017, Eggo consumption saw a 14% year-on-year increase thanks to Stranger Things.

(776) The Duffers say Broadway kids have a habit of ending up in the show. "It's weird, these Broadway kids. I don't know why we keep finding them. But Gaten [Matarazzo] and Caleb [McLaughlin] were both on Broadway, and they actually knew Sadie. Because I guess apparently all the Broadway kids

play on the same playground? I have no idea. There's this little weird group of them, and they're all very, very talented kids. Also, they're incredible singers, so if we ever wanted to do a musical episode, we're good to go."

(777) The first teaser trailer for Stranger Things 2 featured a real 1980 Eggo commercial featuring Wonder Years star Jason Hervey.

(778) When Stranger Things 2 was due for release, a man named Harry Moore made a contract for his girlfriend to sign so that he could avoid spoilers! The contract said - "no episode of Stranger Things Series Two to be consumed in the absence of your partner, all spoilers to be avoided, in the event of a spoiler being discovered it must not be shared with your partner, neither partner may be in the same room as 'Stranger Things Series Two' episode unless with your partner, series one episodes are excluded from this contract."

(779) Noah Schnapp researched possessed people to prepare for season two.

(780) Ross Duffer says that A Nightmare On Elm Street was an important influence on Stranger Things because of the way that an unexplained evil infiltrated the very mundane and ordinary real world. This juxtaposition can be very frightening.

(781) An enterprising fan remixed the Stranger Things theme to see what it would sound like on an 8-bit computer game.

(782) Charlie Heaton says he had almost forgotten about his Stranger Things audition when he was told he had the part. "I went home and kind of forgot about it. But eventually I got a call one night at 4am and it was the Duffer Brothers, and they were like, 'Hey Charlie – we just wanted to let you know we'd like you to play this role! So do you wanna come and play this

role?'"

(783) Natalia Dyer says she was pessimistic about being cast in Stranger Things after her audition. "I actually remember feeling really terrible after the audition and the callback. The day of the audition, I was moving out of my apartment, and I had been crying all morning because I was so stressed. Then I had the audition and was really feeling terrible about it. So, honestly, I was very incredulous about the whole thing until I got the phone call that I got the role, which is great when you don't expect good things to happen."

(784) Finn Wolfhard says the bullies at his school were scared of him after Stranger Things came out.

(785) It took fifteen hair care products before they found the right one to use on Joe Keery for Steve's hair.

(786) The Duffers say that Millie Bobby Brown was a little unsure at first of another girl coming in to join the tight knit younger cast gang in season two. "Millie was very nervous about another girl coming: What is this going to be like? Now they're best friends. She's like, "Thank God for bringing in another girl, because I am so sick of these boys!""

(787) Tiffany's Kitchen, the real life location of Benny's Burgers is ranked #6 of 48 Restaurants in Lithia Springs by TripAdvisor.

(788) Millie Bobby Brown says shaving her hair off for the part of Eleven was inspiring. "The day I shaved my head was the most empowering moment of my whole life. The last strand of hair cut off was the moment my whole face was on show and I couldn't hide behind my hair like I used to."

(789) Natalia Dyer says the TV show she likes the most at the moment is Orange is the New Black.

(790) The Duffers say that Paul Reiser was very quick to accept the offer to play Dr Owens. "We met him at, I think it was at a diner. We hadn't written a single word, and he's like, "Whatever you want to do, I'm in." He was so lovely to deal with."

(791) Hopper's morse code knock at the cabin to Eleven is (• • − / • • •). The translation is "us".

(792) David Harbour says he is looking forward to a future scene where Hopper has to give Mike a 'dad talk'. "The fun thing about the dad aspect of Hopper is going to be how he handles a teenage daughter and her relationship to a boy like Mike. So there may be that conversation where he has to sit Mike down on the couch when he comes calling for the date and she's getting ready, and Hopper will be like 'Sit on the couch − what are your intentions with my daughter?'That scene may be coming in season three. I would relish that, because the amount of difficulty it'd take for Hopper to do that is going to be pretty hysterical."

(793) The Demogorgon was designed to have a prominent silhouette.

(794) Winona is a Sioux Indian name meaning firstborn daughter.

(795) The Duffers say the thought process for the start of season two was this - "You just want to expand it a little bit more. You want new locations, you want new colors, you want new characters. So that's really what episode one is about, just starting to introduce these new flavors and characters into the show."

(796) Ewan McGregor was apparently considered at one point for the part of Hopper.

(797) Shannon Purser says she had no idea if Barb was dead or not after she finished shooting her scenes. "It's really interesting because there was this weird air of secrecy about the seventh episode, which is when we discover Barb's fate. Nobody would tell me what happened. I don't know if they were told not to or whatever, but nobody would talk about it. I had no idea what was going to happen. But by episode three, I knew things were not looking super great for her. It was kind of a waiting game."

(798) Prior to production, the younger cast members started their own group chat they called Stranger Texts.

(799) Millie Bobby Brown says in real life that her lucky number is 8.

(800) When Nancy stabs the possessed Will with the poker in Stranger Things 2, they used the same Will dummy from season one.

(801) Netflix released a virtual reality trailer when the first season came out where you could scroll around the screen and explore the spooky confines of the Christmas light festooned Byers house.

(802) The song When it's Cold by Moby plays as Joyce and Hopper try to revive Will in the Upside Down. This song was also used at the end of The Sopranos episode two, season six.

(803) Shannon Purser tried to return to her movie theatre job but found that fans of Stranger Things were trying to track her down. "People started showing up at work, and I figured maybe I should lay low for a while. But it's been a really good job!"

(804) Both E.T. and Stranger Things feature characters named

Mike and Steve.

(805) The Duffers say they always enjoy doing scenes where Eleven has a telekinetic temper tantrum.

(806) Joe Keery had to do several takes of the scene where Steve eats chicken while with Barb's parents.

(807) Popular Science said it would take 1,183 pounds of salt to make a girl the size and height of Millie Bobby Brown float in a sensory deprivation tank. That was remarkably close to the actual figure used in the scene. It equates to around 24 bags of salt.

(808) The weapon Mike is holding at the end of The Mind Flayer as the Byers house is under siege is a candlestick! Finn Wolfhard apparently chose this weapon.

(809) Shannon Purser says she was covered in bruises after shooting Barb's death scene.

(810) Over 150 wigs were required on set during the production of Stranger Things.

(811) Amy Forsythe, the makeup department head of Stranger Things, suggests that Eleven did her own Snow Ball makeup after learning about makeup during her stay with Kali's gang.

(812) Priah Ferguson improvised the moment where Erica calls Lucas a nerd under her breath.

(813) The shed where Will vanishes in the first episode has an upside down horseshoe above the door, a symbol of bad luck.

(814) Linnea Berthelsen's first name Linnea is a popular Scandinavian name inspired by the renowned botanist Carl Linnaeus.

(815) Gaten Matarazzo says that since Stranger Things came out people at school who used to ignore him now want to be his friend.

(816) Freaks And Geeks and Friday Night Lights, two shows about teen characters, were an underrated influence on Stranger Things. Matt Duffer said - "I thought, 'OK, television now is becoming more cinematic. Can you do a show where you care about the characters just as much as Freaks And Geeks or Friday Night Lights, but can there also please be a monster in it?' So that was a goal with it. I just hadn't seen enough of that on TV."

(817) Charlie Heaton, who is British in real life, was cast as Jonathan because the Duffers couldn't find an American actor who was brooding enough for the part.

(818) Millie Bobby Brown's audition consisted of 'fake' scenes that weren't in the actual script.

(819) Natalia Dyer says she loved wearing the eighties clothes and describes the fashions of that decade as 'whimsical'.

(820) Paul Reiser says that Stranger Things is a very friendly cast and set to join. "It's a very, very friendly group. And I was the new kid on the block. But they were oh so friendly. And even the kids – it's a very huggy group. Even on the first day, they hug you… And it's not showbiz huggy. It's more like, 'Hey, welcome.' The kids have their own tight group. Winona [Ryder] was very, very welcoming. She's delightful. I fell for her, her character… They're all very welcoming and great fun to work with."

(821) Mike and Hopper are the only two characters who feature in every episode in some way.

(822) When asked which one character she would choose to save in season one, Millie Bobby Brown chose the Byers' dog Chester!

(823) You can see some Ritz crackers in the old eighties tin during the scenes at Benny's Burgers.

(824) Winona Ryder says that when she was a teenager a casting director once said she wasn't good looking enough to be an actress.

(825) The Duffers say that working on Wayward Pines under M. Night Shyamalan taught them how to make a television show. "That became our training ground, and M. Night Shyamalan became a great mentor to us. By the time we came out of that show, we were like, 'OK, we know how to put together a show.' And that's when we wrote Stranger Things."

(826) In the scene where Dustin brings some Pringles to Mike's basement, the props department have erroneously supplied a 1968 version of the Pringles tube.

(827) David Harbour says that if he had to cosplay one character it would be Barb.

(828) Joe Keery says that when he was working in a Burger establishment waiting tables and got the good news that he had been cast as Steve in Stranger Things he 'high-fived' a fellow employee in the alley.

(829) Finn Wolfhard was sick when he filmed the Snow Ball scene at the end of season two.

(830) The Duffers say the list of alternative titles for Stranger Things is so bad they'll never release them.

(831) David Harbour wants more development of the

relationship between Hopper and Joyce in future seasons. "I've been pretty vocal about how I love the dynamic between Joyce and Hopper, which I don't feel like we got a lot of time to explore in season two."

(832) Finn Wolfhard named 'Trick or Treat, Freak' as as the episode he likes the best so far from both seasons.

(833) Shawn Levy says that around fifty directors have been rejected for Stranger Things.

(834) Levy says they wanted to avoid 'journeyman' TV directors.

(835) Andrew Stanton reached out to the Stranger Things production and said he was a fan and as Levy and the Duffers loved his Pixar work they allowed him to direct in season two.

(836) David Harbour thinks you don't have to have a rippling six-pack body to be attractive. "If you have a dad bod, if you wear it well, and still shake your hips pretty good, I feel like you too can be a sex symbol."

(837) While at Chapman University, the Duffers made some short films together. One was about a 1666 plague and another was about a cannibal on the loose!

(838) At at a comic con after Stranger Things 2, when asked who she would save out of Hopper and Mike, Millie Bobby Brown said she'd save Hopper. Her reasoning? She said Finn Wolfhard wouldn't be too bothered by her choice but David Harbour on the other hand would be devastated if she didn't choose Hopper!

(839) Steve's famous nail encrusted baseball bat was actually made by Jonathan!

(840) On the set they have both a real nail encrusted bat and also a fake one that is safe to use in action scenes.

(841) At the end of season one, where Joyce, Jonathan and Will sit down to Christmas dinner, there are no Christmas lights. Understandably, they don't want to be reminded of Christmas lights for a long time!

(842) Millie Bobby Brown was named the number one breakout star of 2016 by IMDB.

(843) Among the classic boardgames you can see in the Wheeler basement in season one are Upwords and Score Four.

(844) Johnny Depp used to have a tattoo that said 'Winona Forever'. When he broke up with Winona Ryder he changed it to 'Wino Forever'.

(845) The Duffers say that in the original conception for Stranger Things they toyed with the idea of never showing the Upside Down.

(846) The original episode titles for Stranger Things 2 were released but then later changed. They were - Madmax, The Boy Who Came Back to Life, The Pumpkin Patch, The Palace, The Storm, The Pollywog, The Secret Cabin, The Brain, The Lost Brother.

(847) The Duffers say they changed some of the titles to make them more opaque. They didn't want Reddit detectives to get on the case.

(848) You can see tins of Sun-Maid Raisons in the Wheeler basement with the classic tin.

(849) Millie Bobby Brown says her most emotional scene to shoot was when Eleven encounters a vision of Brenner in The

Lost Sister.

(850) The Duffers say that they auditioned literally 'everyone' for the part of Steve.

(851) Cara Buono says that when she read the script for Stranger Things she called her agent and said that she was desperate to be in the show.

(852) The character of Dustin is the only one of the boys in the show not to have a brother or sister.

(853) Scientist Marius Stan said the further dimensions might possibly exist and scientific experiments on the subject are ongoing. "They are smashing particles against each other at very high energy. They hope to create mini black holes with very high density of matter — even light can't get out of that. By doing that, they want to prove theories that say our universe is, in fact multidimensional, has more than three or four dimensions we are used to."

(854) Mike Wheeler is the first character who refers to the Upside Down.

(855) Millie Bobby Brown says her most beloved fashion brands are Burberry, Stella McCartney and Coach.

(856) Natalia Dyer says she would love Nancy to have more scenes with the kids.

(857) The smiley faced yellow yo-yo used by Jonathan and Nancy to set a trap for the Demogorgon in season one is a reference to the smiley face in Joe Dante's The Howling.

(858) Shawn Levy says the Duffers allowed more camera movement in season two. In season one the camera moves were minimal to mimic eighties films and TV.

(859) In 2016, Stranger Things was the top original digital show in the United States, Japan, Great Britain, Australia, France, Germany, and Sweden.

(860) In 2016, a website called TheStudioExec.com reported that Stephen King was going to write the second season of Stranger Things. This turned out to be an example of what we would call fake news. It was a false report.

(861) Millie Bobby Brown says she relates more to the Eleven of season two because she shows more emotion.

(862) Video game designer and BASIC coder Lance McDonald, in a lengthy Twitter post, defended the scene in The Mind Flayer where Bob puts the lab security back online using BASIC computer code from critics. "I was just annoyed at how many people are like 'THIS IS THE DUMBEST SCENE IN STRANGER THINGS YOU CANT RESET A BREAKER WITH BASIC CODE' like as if this was some CSI; Cyber level s***. He's just writing a brute force password retriever on an interpreter that would be on EVERY computer in that era. It's a good scene."

(863) In Stranger Things 2, we see that Dustin has a Wheel of Fortune board game in his house.

(864) The Duffers say that when Finn Wolfhard did his Skype audition they ended up spending most of the time talking about movies with him.

(865) Joe Keery's audition involved the scene where Steve smashes Jonathan's camera.

(866) In early rehearsals for the show, Stranger Things creators Matt and Ross Duffer told Millie Bobby Brown that she was basically going to "be an alien."

(867) Lucas using the slingshot against the monster at the end of season one is taken from Stephen King's It.

(868) When Charlie Heaton presented a gong at a British TV awards show in 2018, viewers were surprised to learn he was British as they only really knew him from Stranger Things where, of course, he plays an American.

(869) The Duffers say that Finn Wolfhard, out of the kids, reminds them the most of themselves when they were that age.

(870) The boys (Finn, Lucas, Gaten) say they want Nancy to end up with Jonathan ('Jancy') while Millie Bobby Brown prefers 'Stancy' and wants Nancy to be with Steve.

(871) When Bob Newby says "What's at the X, pirate treasure?" in Stranger things 2, this is an obvious reference to The Goonies.

(872) You can see some Jif Peanut Butter in the Wheeler kitchen in the first season in the classic glass jar.

(873) Despite all the real life food and drink products in the show, the Duffers say there is no official product placement in Stranger Things. "Someone has to give permission, but if you're using the product in the appropriate way, it's an easy ok. But it's not like we're working hand-in-hand with these companies You don't want product placement. You want it to be about what would these kids actually be into. For season 2 with Eggo there was some cooperation, but no, they had no idea it [was going to be] in the show."

(874) When Steve is eating in the school cafeteria in season one with Nancy, Tommy and Carol, they are drinking a Freeland Dairy orange drink.

(875) The swing on the Byers' porch is a nod to Sam Raimi's The Evil Dead.

(876) When Billy is lifting weights in The Spy the music video on television is Ratt performing Round and Round from the album Out of the Cellar.

(877) In 2018 a Kickstarter campaign was launched to bring back some classic Dungeons & Dragons figurines seen in Stranger Things.

(878) The Duffers decided not to call the Upside Down its original name of the Nether when people made jokes about nether regions.

(879) When Murray Bauman has the vodka in Stranger Things 2, the label seems to be incorrect. SLOTichnaya instead of STOLichnaya.

(880) The Stranger Things kids watched the Superbowl teaser for Stranger Things 2 together and got quite excited.

(881) A band called Greg In Good Company released a song named Monster's Lair which was inspired by Joyce Byers in Stranger Things.

(882) Millie Bobby Brown says she finds it a bit strange to see grown men cosplaying Eleven.

(883) Dustin brings some Bazooka bubble gum as part of his food package when the boys decide to search for Will again. This brand of bubble gum was first marketed in 1947.

(884) In season one you can see some Tab in the Wheeler basement. This was one of the very first sugar free soft drinks.

(885) Other board games we see in the Wheeler basement are Family Feud and Dungeon.

(886) Joe Keery says he hated how 'self-absorbed' Steve was in season one.

(887) Matt Duffer was amazed by the performance of Noah Schnapp in Stranger Things 2. "I didn't know he was this amazing. He blew everyone away and surprised everybody."

(888) Joyce buys 'Santa-Trim' Christmas lights in season one.

(889) Joe Keery says he learned a lot about acting from the kids in the show.

(890) David Harbour says of Hopper the parent that "I really don't want to become the dad from Full House who's always adorable but kind of loses his own personhood."

(891) Dacre Montgomery asked the Duffers for some sort of context as to why Billy was was so horrible. He was relieved to therefore to get the scene where Billy's father is shown to be intimidating and violent to Billy.

(892) In 2017, clothing retailer Top Shop rebranded its Oxford Street shop in London into a Stranger Things themed branch to celebrate the return of the show.

(893) Finn Wolfhard says that in season two "I wasn't really in Mike mode until the end of episode three. By the end of the season, everything was a little more normal ... for him."

(894) At the Stranger Things 2 premiere, the Hawkins Fair themed party served corn dogs, funnel cakes, fresh donuts, and cocktails such as the UpCider Down, the Maple Bourbon Bone Chiller, and Pumpkin Ale.

(895) Waitresses at the Stranger Things 2 premiere were dressed in eggo yellow uniforms.

(896) Joe Keery says the secret of his hair is the 'genetics' of his parents.

(897) Shawn Levy says a 'big sci-fi idea' was dropped from season two but may be used in the future.

(898) Brett Gelman says "Murray is like the Richard Dreyfuss character in Jaws. He's trying to wake up this sleepy town."

(899) When Steve and the kids take refuge in the bus in the junkyard this might be another reference to the Mad Max film series - where vehicles are fortified to survive in a post apocalyptic future. MADMAX is - as we have mentioned - the username of Max in the arcade.

(900) Stranger Things 2 broke a Twitter record, with users have generating more than 3.7 million tweets about the show.

(901) Dan Aykroyd says he was happy to give permission for Ghostbusters uniforms to be worn in Stranger Things when he and Ivan Reitman were asked. "Well they are just such fans of the Ghostbusters in the show, and it fits perfectly for the timeline of their show. So I believe it was really just a result of how they had linked up our movie with the second season. It just seemed to be a fantastic tie-in and a beautiful nostalgic tie-in as well. So the guys in Stranger Things, essentially they are the Ghostbusters in elementary school."

(902) Aykroyd said he enjoyed the show and wafted away the thought of doing a cameo. "I don't think so. Don't think so. Anything's possible, but I don't think they need me, or any Ghostbusters from the movie. They're doing really really well with their stories and they're beautifully shot, beautifully written, and I've been enjoying. In my research on this, I had

to watch many of them and I've been enjoying my research."

(903) The Duffer Brothers were wary of doing the possession storyline with Will since it had been done so many times before.

(904) You can see some vintage Hershey's cocoa powder in the police station in season one.

(905) Priah Ferguson is being upgraded to full cast member for season three.

(906) David Harbour says of life on the Stranger Things set with the kids that - "Sometimes when they get a little out of hand, I also am the guy who's able to be on set saying, "All right, come on kids, let's get down to work." So in some ways I'm a cool uncle, and in some ways I'm like a nasty physics teacher."

(907) Gaten Matarazzo says it was his idea to open season two in an arcade.

(908) Yet more Stranger Things products now available include a Demogorgon dog hat, a 'Where's Barb?' book, and an Upside Down Snow Globe.

(909) For the season two marketing, Netflix released a YouTube playlist called Hawkins Monitored where you could spy on various characters through surveillance footage.

(910) Season one had one computer effects expert but they had a full special effects team for season 2.

(911) Matt Duffer says the Snow Ball scene took two days to shoot.

(912) David Harbour says he auditioned to play supervillain

The Blob in X-Men Origins: Wolverine but didn't get the part because they thought he was too fat!

(913) Despite dressing up as Michael Myers for the Halloween night scenes in Stranger Things 2, Sadie Sink had no idea who Michael Myers was.

(914) In season one, the Duffers persuaded Netflix to give them some more money to spend on episode eight so they could make it as good as it could possibly be.

(915) Shawn Levy says pairing David Harbour and Millie Bobby Brown was the 'Clash of the Titans'. "You've got power going against power."

(916) For New York comic con, twenty Dustin lookalikes on pedicabs were dispatched to the streets blasting eighties music.

(917) Dacre Montgomery says Billy swore more in the original Stranger Things 2 scripts but his language was toned down.

(918) There has been Stranger Things Minecraft and Stranger Things Lego.

(919) Should you desire, you can now buy an eggo waffle stereo holder.

(920) Shawn Levy says it was relatively easy to get the clearance to use Dragon's Lair.

(921) Levy says that getting the clearance to use Michael Myers and his Halloween mask on the other hand was much more difficult.

(922) Levy calls the producer's role on Stranger Things a "nightmare of clearances."

(923) "There are definitely similarities between Bob and Samwise," said Sean Astin. "Sam is the guy you want to have with you when stuff gets hard. As it turns out, even though he's a dorky wannabe stepdad, Bob is also a guy who isn't overwhelmed by a terrifying reality."

(924) Finn Wolfhard's bedridden audition was not even in focus.

(925) When Eleven wants to go trick or treating in season two she puts a sheet over her head so she can go as a ghost and won't be seen. This is the same outfit ET wears during Halloween in E.T. the Extra-Terrestrial.

(926) Will the Wise, an episode title in season two, is a character Will created in season one. A fantasy wizard.

(927) A shrine to Barb was created by fans at a 2017 Comic Con.

(928) The Demogorgon was fully CGI when being hit by rocks in the classroom in the first season finale.

(929) In the episode Trick or Treat, Freak we learn that Eleven was only trapped in the Upside Down for a matter of minutes after the end of the first season finale.

(930) The Duffers say that their direction notes in season one included reminders to the obstreperous kids not to slap each other before takes!

(931) Kellogs celebrated the return of Stranger Things by releasing 9 Eggo recipes, inspired by episode titles.

(932) Ross Duffer said it was unavoidable that Bob had to die. "This is not a kids show — there are consequences, and people

do die."

(933) Matt Duffer said this of the departed Bob - "I have some Bob ideas, but I don't know what to do with him. I will say I would love to revisit the character… in some way, but I don't know how to even do that."

(934) Susan Shalhoub Larkin, who plays Florence, is the sister of Monk star Tony Shalhoub.

(935) When shooting the emotional classroom showdown in the last episode of season one, the kids apparently found it hard not to laugh.

(936) Shawn Levy says that the relative inexperience of the Duffers made them more 'audacious' on Stranger Things. They didn't follow any set rules.

(937) Shawn Levy says that ideas for season two were already being discussed before the first season had even been released.

(938) The extras at the Snow Ball dance applauded after Finn Wolfhard and Millie Bobby Brown shot their kissing scene.

(939) The Snow Ball dance was always earmarked as the 'end destination' of season two right from the start of the writing process.

(940) The kissing scene with Max and Lucas at the Snow Ball had to be shot more than once because the camera didn't pick up the reaction of Caleb McLaughlin at first.

(941) The scene was the first kiss both onscreen or in real life for both Sadie Sink and Caleb McLaughlin.

(942) When Millie Bobby Brown came up with Eleven's flick of the head to indicate she'd violently snapped someone's neck,

Matthew Modine was apparently quite shocked to see her display so much glee at the invention!

(943) Video arcade historians don't think that Asteroids would have really been in the (rather spangly) Palace Arcade. Asteroids came out in 1979 and so would have been an old machine even in 1984.

(944) Fabergé Organics had a range of Farrah Fawcett endorsed hair products (shampoo, conditioner, and hairspray) in the seventies and early eighties but the line was discontinued in 1984 after a change of ownership in the company.

(945) Millie Bobby Brown thinks that Brenner isn't as bad as he seems. She shares this view with Matthew Modine.

(946) Shawn Levy says it only occurred to them after they had wrapped on Stranger Things 2 how big a role puzzles play in the plot.

(947) Both seasons of Stranger Things have 94% on Rotten Tomatoes.

(948) Phil Callahan, the police officer at the Hawkins Police Department, may be a reference to Father Callahan, a Stephen King character from Salem's Lot and the Dark Tower.

(949) Some retro gamers have said that Eleven's dress and wig costume from season one is similar to Paula, a character in the 1994 Super Nintendo classic Earthbound. Paula even has psychokinetic powers too.

(950) When Eleven is in the Ives house, a channel cuts to Action 8 News to foreshadow Kali.

(951) In the first season you see a yellow Ford Festiva. This car

didn't come out until 1986.

(952) You can see some Wonder Bread in the Byers kitchen in season one. Wonder Bread was launched in 1921. It was the first American bread brand to feature open dating as well as nutrition information on its packaging

(953) Caleb McLaughlin says the most difficult part of being famous is having to constantly be careful of what you say and what you do because you are now in the public eye and subject to constant scrutiny.

(954) When Stranger Things 2 was released, Millie Bobby Brown performed a Stranger Things season one recap rap on The Tonight Show.

(955) Bellwood Quarry also appears in the Netflix movie The Fundamentals of Caring.

(956) When Steve and Billy are on the basketball court in Stranger Things 2, the real life coach who trained the actors is playing the coach in the background.

(957) Priah Ferguson says she loves the blunt attitude of Erica and the fact that she says what is on her mind.

(958) David Harbour says that - "The only thing I think about all my audiences is that they are smarter than me, funnier than me, more emotionally deep than me. And so I'm trying to reach them with my best, my funniest, my subtlest."

(959) The cast and crew are generally agreed that it would be fun to see Mrs Wheeler and Billy become involved in some way.

(960) You can now buy a Funko Pop Demogorgon toy!

(961) Gaten Matarazzo had no idea that he wasn't competing with anyone for the part of Dustin.

(962) Eggo waffles were known as Froffles when they first appeared in supermarket freezers.

(963) Reese's Pieces were called PBs when they were first launched.

(964) Using Reese's Pieces in E.T was the idea of a vice president at the film studio. He'd asked his son which candy E.T might be tempted by.

(965) At just eleven years-old, Gaten Matarazzo was performing 6 days a week and matinees for his role of Gavroche in Les Misérables - all while still attending school!

(966) The Stranger things title sequence is inspired by the titles for 1984's The Terminator.

(967) Caleb McLaughlin says he would love to be in a Marvel film.

(968) A demographic breakdown for Stranger Things showed it was very popular with females as women and girls accounted for 57% of the audience.

(969) Millie Bobby Brown has already appeared on around twenty magazine front covers.

(970) The research of Netflix on viewing habits of Stranger Things found that the second episode was the one that 'hooked' viewers. Those who made it to the second episode overwhelmingly went on to watch the rest of the season.

(971) Ham radio is still used by some two million licensed operators all over the world.

(972) When Hopper is with Joyce outside the Snow Ball dance he was originally going to be wearing a tie but the Duffers decided to remove this. David Harbour said - "Someone (online) caught me in an off-camera thing and I have a tie on. The idea was perhaps that Hopper even puts on a tie for the first time in 20 years to bring his adopted daughter to this dance. So I think Hopper put a lot of effort and work into it."

(973) Eleven was much more feral in the pilot script. When she sneaks into Benny's diner she bites into a fish she finds in the fridge and we see her violently dispatch the agents in the kitchen after they kill Benny.

(974) In the pilot script, Ted Wheeler is trying to watch CHiPS rather than Knight Rider.

(975) In the pilot script, Benny Hammond was called Benny Henderson, implying that he was originally intended to be a possible relation to Dustin.

(976) The music that plays in the music box Eleven opens in the Wheeler house is Brahms' Lullaby.

(977) Eleven's age is not stated but it is suggested she is twelve in season one because that's how long Terry Ives has been looking for her.

(978) The kids had to be tutored on the set during season one and say they bonded over algebra.

(979) Millie Bobby Brown says that in season one when she had finished her own scenes she would sneak back onto the set to watch Winona Ryder work.

(980) Sadie Sink's favourite documentary is Black Fish.

(981) Lucas was called Lucas Conley in the Stranger Things pilot script.

(982) Millie Bobby Brown had a comical response when asked what she thought happened to Eleven after she vanished in a cloud of dust in the first season finale. "Eleven goes to LA, you know, she has a super famous boyfriend. She lives in a mansion, she forgets about Mike, you know, who is he?"

(983) A filmed scene in season one of Eleven reading Nancy's diary in the Wheeler house was cut.

(984) In the pilot script, Mike has a crush on Jennifer Hayes - the girl seen mourning at Will's 'funeral'.

(985) The typewriter seen in Hopper's office is a IBM Selectric III.

(986) Benny has a Rottweiler dog in the pilot script.

(987) The pills Hopper is popping in episode one are Tuinal - a sedative and anti-anxiety pill.

(988) Chris Trujillo says it was difficult to prepare the Byers house interior set for shooting because it was frequently wrecked!

(989) Winona Ryder's agent told her not to act in Heathers and warned it would ruin her career.

(990) David Harbour says he thinks Hopper is not as safe as you might think - "I will be the first to tell you, Hopper is not safe, Hopper is very, very killable, and he doesn't always make the best decisions, like going into tunnels without backup, things like that. The fundamental aspect of Hopper's personality is that he's not about self-preservation, he's about justice. He's not even about personal happiness, he's about

justice. So he's willing to sacrifice himself for the greater good and so that is something that... he is definitely killable. I don't want him to get killed, but that's all up to the Duffer brothers, you know?"

(991) David Harbour says the worst thing about being in the Upside Down in season one was that the Hazmat suits they wore took half an hour to take off before you could use the bathroom!

(992) David Harbour often played villains in the past and tapped into this experience when he took on the more heroic role of Hopper. "I often seek contradiction to any known trope I play. In A Walk Among the Tombstones, I play a horrible man – a truly dark villain – and it was important to me that he was as human as possible, that he could make you laugh and charm you a little. It makes it that much scarier when we laugh with that person because through laughter we identify, and identifying with 'Ray' was not a pleasant thing to do. In a similar fashion, since I knew Hop was so heroic, I sought out the areas of him that were broken, messed up and 'bad' (these monikers may seem trite, but in the lexicon of heroes and villains they are what we have). You don't have to like a hero at the beginning of a story, you just have to pay attention to him or her. I would even say that the journey with Hop becomes more satisfying if you don't like him at the beginning and you write him off as callous and a jerk. Then, you get to uncover what's behind that and can love him all the more. People that have it all together are hard to love; because they don't need our love, they will be fine without us. Hop needs your love because he is not okay; he is broken, and he may not make the right decisions. It's a rich journey."

(993) David Harbour says his perfect breakfast is - "Coffee and a nice, hot everything bagel with cream cheese, tomato, a little onion and a healthy dose of salt and pepper."

(994) In the pilot script, Benny's Burgers was a Fish and Chip themed diner.

(995) In the pilot script it is Lucas who has a crush on Mike's sister Nancy rather than Dustin.

(996) Joyce drops a lot of f-bombs in the pilot script.

(997) The Duffers say that most of the networks who rejected Stranger Things wanted it to be more like Twin Peaks.

(998) Charlie Heaton says he usually tends to get cast in dark brooding roles. "I tend to get drawn to dark roles. When I'm looking for a role, I always have to find something true that's in myself that I can put into the role. I'm not saying I'm really dark or anything, but it's about finding that vulnerability. Everyone has vulnerabilities that they maybe don't want to share. You find yourself being drawn to characters that are somehow similar to yourself or have gone through things that you're going through or you can relate to them somehow."

(999) Winona Ryder was given the middle name Laura because of her parents' friendship with Laura Huxley, writer Aldous Huxley's wife.

(1000) Millie Bobby Brown says she is still scared of the dark despite her heroics in Stranger Things. "I never liked sleeping in the dark. I have, like, twinkle stars around my bed, so it's not so bad."

Manufactured by Amazon.ca
Bolton, ON